JOSÉ SILVA'S
CHOOSE
SUCCESS
MASTER COURSE

JOSÉ SILVA'S
CHOOSE
SUCCESS
MASTER COURSE

UNLEASH YOUR GENIUS MIND
Original Edition

José Silva
with **Ed Bernd Jr.**

MEDIA

Published 2022 by Gildan Media LLC
aka G&D Media
www.GandDmedia.com

First Edition: 2022

Front Cover design by David Rheinhardt of Pyrographx

Interior design by Meghan Day Healey of Story Horse, LLC.

Library of Congress Cataloging-in-Publication Data is available upon request

ISBN: 978-1-7225-0597-4

10   9   8   7   6   5   4   3   2   1

Contents

ONE
Your Mind Holds the Secret to Success 1

TWO
Using the Powerful Alpha Brain Wave Level 19

THREE
Sleep Control, To Awake Control, and Awake Control 25

FOUR
Programmed Dreams and Headache Control 37

FIVE
The Mental Screen and Memory Pegs 49

SIX
The Three Fingers Technique,
Speed Learning, and Test Taking 61

SEVEN
Unleash Your Genius Mind: Visualization and
Imagination to Solve Problems and Create Solutions 69

EIGHT

Hand Levitation and Glove Anesthesia   91

NINE

Mental Rehearsal for Better Performance   103

TEN

Stop Bad Habits and Start Good New Ones   111

ELEVEN

Call on Expert Help Whenever You Need It   123

TWELVE

Your Next Step: Developing Your God-Given ESP   135

Appendix A

The Silva Centering Exercise by José Silva   145

Appendix B

Forty-Day Countdown System
for Finding the Alpha Level   157

Appendix C

Conditioning Cycle to Use
When Impressing Formulas   165

Appendix D

Hand Levitation and Glove Anesthesia
Conditioning Cycle   187

Appendix E

Resources and Contact Information   197

ONE

Your Mind Holds the Secret to Success

Thank you for choosing to learn José Silva's Choose Success Master Course. The coursework—the Silva Centering Exercise and all of the Formula-Type Techniques—were authored by José Silva. The explanations and examples are mine, Ed Bernd Jr. They were approved by José Silva himself. Welcome aboard, and let's get started.

Until now, your chances of achieving great success were more a matter of luck of the draw than intelligence, skill, enthusiasm, hard work, persistence, and all the other things that the writers of success books write about.

If you're like me, you've probably read a lot of self-improvement books, attended a lot of seminars, listened to a thousand and one audiotapes, watched people tell their miracle stories on television . . . and you're still searching for something that will help *you* the way that other people claim to have been helped by all those other programs.

The truth is that only about one person in ten gets any real results from those programs because nine out of ten people are able to think with only their left brain hemisphere. Approximately one person in ten is able to think with their right brain hemisphere, and then act with their left brain hemisphere.

How much does it help to be able to use two brain hemispheres instead of just one? Imagine this: How it would be if most people thought that they could only use one leg. If everybody else hopped around on one leg, while you used two legs, you could get around much faster and easier than they could. That's what it's like when you use two brains instead of just one. That's why some people—the super successful people—seem to have so much more ability than the average person.

The good news is that you can now learn to use both brain hemispheres to think with—you can learn to use more of your brain and mind than the average person so that you will have the ability to achieve great success also.

This means that from now on you can achieve even greater success in everything you do.

Millions of people in 103 countries around the world have already benefited, and now you will too.

Research on the effectiveness of the Silva techniques has proven that no matter how much—or how little—success you've had up until now, you will benefit.

Single mothers on welfare benefited.

So did executives at RCA Records.

And adolescent inner-city students.

And alcoholics.

And regular people like you and me.

But the main question is: What does it take for you to be successful—with this course, and in life?

First, you have to want it. You have to want to be successful. So let's talk about your reasons for taking the course.

Maybe your reasons are personal, for yourself.

Maybe you want to help your family . . .

Maybe career . . .

Recreational activities . . .

What do you want?

How will it help you?

Why is that important to you?

To increase your desire, think of all the benefits you will derive.

Who else will benefit?

The more people who will benefit, the greater your desire.

José Silva says that we are not here just to live it up, we're not here for a seventy-year coffee break. We have a purpose, and that purpose is to solve problems, relieve suffering, and improve living conditions on the planet.

Your obligation is to be the best that you can be—the best parent, the best spouse, the best employee, employer, or whatever your obligations are.

It is important to focus on your reasons for taking this Master Course and to increase your desire.

Because then, with every technique, you will be thinking about how it can help you to correct problems and achieve your goals.

It is important for another reason too:

When you learn to enter deep levels of mind, which you will begin to do in this home study course, when you go deep within yourself, you will be carrying that desire there with you, and that desire, at those deep inner levels, will produce results.

Whenever you talk with people, that deep inner desire to help them will express itself.

Fives Steps to Success

We'll build towards outstanding success in five steps. Sort of like building a pyramid. The foundation—the base of our pyramid—is how you use your mind:

Functioning at the alpha brain wave level.

Positive thinking / attitude / belief systems.

The second block in our pyramid is self-management. You will learn techniques to help you deal with problems like insomnia, tension and migraine headaches, poor memory, and bad habits. You need to prepare the vehicle. It is not enough to just have correct attitudes and beliefs; you also need specific tools to help you get your life in order so that you can enjoy the success that you deserve.

You want that perfect job, that ideal mate; you want to help bring peace to the planet. First, do whatever you must do to take control of your own life. How can you be a successful and important businessperson if you have headaches every day? If you have debilitating habits?

The third step deals with communications and decision making. You will learn strategies to obtain information and then use that information to make the best possible decisions.

Step four puts your decisions into action. Once you have prepared yourself—prepared the vehicle, so to speak—and have made the best possible decisions, then you will be able to program for your goals with complete confidence and full power, knowing that you are on the right track. You will learn several powerful programming techniques for the fourth block of our pyramid to success.

The peak of the pyramid, the pinnacle, is the ability to use intuition to get information and to solve problems. We'll talk about your options for doing that in the final chapter of this Master Course.

How to Use More of Your Mind

For now, let's go back to our foundation: how you use your mind. Albert Einstein recognized the importance of the mind. He said that imagination is more important than knowledge.

Einstein claimed that he used only 10 percent of his mind, and the general public uses only about 3 or 4 percent. And that's what the Silva Courses are all about: learning to use more of your mind.

There is no limit to how far you can go, there is no limit to what you can do, because there is no limit to the power of your mind.

Students report simple things like: stop smoking, fall asleep without drugs and wake up without clocks, relieve nervousness, stop excessive drinking, memorize long lists and improve creativity—to the more sophisticated things like develop ESP and using dreams to solve problems and get information.

The most important key to using more of your mind is learning to function with conscious awareness at the alpha level.

How Your Brain and Mind Work

What exactly is the alpha level? The alpha level is a level associated with relaxation and with light sleep at night. It is associated with daydreaming during the day.

Your brain functions on a small amount of electricity. That electricity pulses or vibrates at different rates, from twenty times per second (known as cycles per second, or cps) when you are wide awake, all the way to one-half a cycle per second in deepest sleep.

This chart is a map of your body, brain, and mind, and how each is functioning as you go through those brain wave levels.

SCALE OF BRAIN EVOLUTION

© Copyright 1969-2001 by Jose Silva & Silva UltraMind Systems, LLC, Laredo, Texas U.S.A.

PHYSICAL WORLD		
SIGHT SOUND SMELL TASTE TOUCH	21 BETA	OUTER CONSCIOUS LEVELS
TIME SPACE	14	
MENTAL WORLD NO TIME | SPACE ESP	ALPHA -CENTER-	INNER CONSCIOUS LEVELS
	7 THETA	
CONNECTION WITH HIGHER INTELLIGENCE	4 DELTA	UNCONSCIOUS

ACTION   SLEEP THOUGHT

Brain Rhythm (Cycles per sec.)

The Delta Doorway to the spiritual dimension

You go through all those levels every night when you sleep.

The key is learning to use the alpha level with conscious awareness—not just reach that level while daydreaming, but being able to activate your mind, to analyze information, and to search for solutions.

You learn to convert the subconscious into an *inner conscious* level.

You learn to do that in a series of mental training exercises—conditioning cycles—where you first learn to relax and then to activate your mind while remaining at the alpha level.

How do you do that? We will give you three options you can choose from. First, though, let's cover two more important points that will help you gain the most benefit from your time at the alpha brain wave level.

Mental Housecleaning

We want to make sure that you are using these powerful alpha levels correctly, because whatever you think about your brain will attempt to produce.

One thing we do is to use a positive thinking technique that we call Mental Housecleaning.

It is based on the idea that your brain functions much like a computer. You can store information in your memory banks, and you can retrieve that information and use it to solve problems.

Many people misunderstand positive thinking. It is simply thinking about what you want, rather than what you don't want.

During the day, notice what you think about, and notice what you say.

Do you imagine yourself having a difficult time getting appointments, or do you imagine yourself making presentations to a lot of people?

Here are some words and phrases that you want to eliminate from your vocabulary, followed by the positive word or phrase to replace them:

- Negative > positive
- I can't > I'll figure out how . . .
- That makes me sick > I dislike that
- I don't think so > I think . . .
- I forgot > It slipped my mind
- I'm a failure > I'm making progress
- I'm shy > I'm confident
- I'm not very smart > I am smart
- I don't feel worthy > I am worthy
- That's a pain in the neck > I can handle this
- I'm afraid > I am confident

Here is what to do when you notice that you are using negative words and phrases:

Stop, and cancel out the negative words by saying: "Cancel-cancel." Then replace the negative words with positive words.

It is very important to always finish with a positive statement, a positive thought.

A fifty-five-year old man who attended the Silva training in Albuquerque, New Mexico, had this to say after reflecting on his language: "For years I've used the phrases, 'I can't see that,' 'It's a pain in the neck,' and 'It's a pain in the . . .' I won't finish the last phrase, but let me explain: I wear glasses, I have headaches in the back of my head, and I have hemorrhoids!"

That got a laugh from the other members of the seminar, but when a person has suffered with those problems for several decades, it is no joke.

A Secret Way to Protect Yourself from Negativity

Sometimes you might find yourself in a situation where you cannot say, "Cancel-cancel." For instance, what do you do if your employer says something negative to you? If you tell them, "Cancel-cancel," they might just cancel-cancel you!

Instead, just give them a big zero. In a computer, the program uses either a zero or a one: That is, the circuit is either open or closed. When it is open, nothing gets through.

So give their negative words a big zero by saying, "Oh."

For example:

"You really fouled up this time!"

"Oh? Well, what can I do to make it right?"

By doing that, you are canceling out the negative thought and replacing it with a positive thought.

Do you want a life filled with success and happiness? You can have it. The choice is yours.

Look for the Good and Praise It

There's a story told about Christopher Columbus sailing his ships east, searching for India. His goal was a continent with untold riches. He sailed on faith and somehow managed to keep his crew under control.

But his first sighting was not of a continent. First he saw some branches and twigs floating in the water.

Did he think that he had failed when his goal was a continent, but all he found were twigs?

Far from it. He viewed the twigs as a sign of progress. If tree branches were floating in the water, could land be far away?

The discovery empowered him and gave him renewed faith and energy.

Remember, when you are working on your projects, as long as you are making progress, you are moving in the correct direction. Keep going. Never give up. You cannot fail . . . unless you quit. If you are not getting positive feedback, then adjust your direction. But always keep going.

We remember Columbus because he kept going until he reached his goal. By doing that, he also demonstrated that the world is not flat and you won't sail off the edge.

Set your goals, make your plans, then keep going.

Rejection Did Not Mean Failure

Let me give you a real-life example:

After my dad retired from a lifetime in the newspaper business, he wanted to stay busy, so he did some public relations work for a group of people who were putting together a seminar on business brokerage.

He prepared ads, wrote stories, and wrote a manual for them. Then, at the last minute, they dropped the project.

He had all this material, so he decided to put it together into a book. He submitted proposals to several book publishers, but they all turned him down. Some of them turned him down because they had just contracted for similar books.

He was choosing to interpret circumstances as failure.

I chose to view them as near success. "There must be land nearby!"

My approach was to "Look for the good and praise it."

I suggested another publisher to him, he sent them the proposal, and they bought it.

He was thrilled. As a newspaper editor, he had won many awards, but he said that getting this book published was the greatest accomplishment of his professional life.

More Information Is Available at Alpha

As we go through this home study course, you will learn how to use your level to obtain information to guide you. You program, you work on a project, and you notice the results. Those results will guide you, so that you know you are on the right track.

The third step in our pyramid to success is learning to obtain information so that you can make correct decisions.

Because when you *know* that you have made the correct decision, you can put all of your energies into achieving your goal.

Back in the 1950s, when I was growing up, Walt Disney created a character based on Davy Crockett. Davy's slogan, according to Disney, was: "Be sure you're right, and then go ahead!"

The Real "Secret" to José Silva's Success

Now there's one more plank in our foundation. So far we have covered:

- The importance of functioning at alpha.
- Mental housecleaning—positive thinking.
- Looking for success—look for the good and praise it.

There is one more issue to address before we learn to use the Silva Centering Exercise to get to the alpha level.

We will teach you how to function at the alpha level; we'll provide the formulas, and show you how to use them. I want to do something more than that:

I want to share with you the secret that José Silva learned through his research that is the key to all great success, happiness, and satisfaction. I'm going to give you the secret that will make all of these techniques in the Silva Systems really work for you.

What José Silva realized, as he worked with thousands of people, studying both the unsuccessful and the successful people, was that a correct sense of values is an important factor in success.

In fact, this was very important to Mr. Silva in his work as a holistic faith healer. He was a very successful healer.

Here is what he wrote in his autobiography about the necessity for a correct sense of values:

> I would ask the patient some questions, such as, "Do you really want to be healed?" and I would add, "because my time is very valuable and I do not intend to waste it." Of course the answer was, "Yes, I want to be healed." Some even felt insulted by my asking such a question. My next question was, "Why do you want to be healed?" If the answer was, "To be a better wife (or husband, or son, or daughter) and help by being a perfect human being who will help solve the problems of my neighborhood, my city, state, or nation," there was no more to say. I would go to work and help the patient. But if the answer centered on how the patient needed to live it up, enjoy life, not helping anything or anybody, then I would try to straighten out the patient's way of thinking before starting the healing.

I realize that not everybody is ready to accept all of these ideas. That's fine. Feel free to study them, and take as long as you need. You can accept or reject anything I say at any time. Or you have another option: put it on a "mental shelf," and come back to it gain later when you have more information and experience.

Once you learn to analyze information while at the alpha level, these ideas will make more sense to you.

Mr. Silva believes that it is very important that we understand what's really important in life.

He tells a story about two neighbors in his hometown of Laredo, Texas, who got into a silly argument that had tragic consequences.

How a Chicken Ruined Two Families

Let's get him to tell us the story about two neighbors of his in Laredo years ago who got into a silly argument that had tragic consequences:

> One neighbor had a little garden in the back yard. The other neighbor had some chickens. One day, one of the chickens jumped the fence and damaged some of the plants in the neighbor's garden.
>
> The two women got into an argument about the damage that had been done. Should there have been a better fence? Was the homeowner responsible for the actions of the chicken?
>
> When the two husbands got home at dinner time, both of the wives were upset and wanted their respective husbands to take some kind of action.

The two men got into an argument . . . which led to one shooting and killing the other.

What a tragedy! One husband dead, the other sent to prison, two women having to raise children alone, the children deprived of their fathers, loss of two wage earners. The tragic consequences go on and on.

We must learn to put things into perspective, and focus on what's really important.

What Is Important?

It is important for us to fulfill our mission in life. And I submit for your consideration that your mission seems to be to correct problems and help make our world a better place to live.

Why do we feel that way? Two reasons:

1. Our observations of successful people.
2. People who follow this path experience success.

I know people who put themselves at the center of their world. I know people who work twenty hours a day, who keep their eye focused on their goal and let nothing dissuade them, people who are willing to win at any cost. I've seen them make a lot of money, but the money didn't make them happy.

I'm not saying that money keeps you from being happy. I also know people who are constantly doing for others, sacrificing, giving and giving. These people never have enough for themselves, and they aren't very happy either. They feel they have been short-changed, and in a sense, they have.

We must always have a balance.

There is a relationship between what we give and what we get.

José Silva's Formula for Prosperity and Abundance

Program to correct problems and make the world a better place to live, and keep in mind what your needs are . . . plus a little bit more.

Let's look at a practical example: Suppose you want to buy or sell a house. You contact some real estate agents. The first agent who comes to see you is desperate for money: they will do anything to make that commission, even if it is not in your best interest.

The second agent is determined to make the best deal for all concerned, even if it takes a little longer, and even if it means a slightly lower commission.

Which one do you want to deal with? Which one has your best interest at heart? Which one are you going to refer to your friends? Who is going to end up with the most customers? The selfish one, or the selfless one? You know the answer.

Sometimes, from an analytical, beta brain wave perspective, it may seem as though we should be trying to get everything we can for ourselves. But from an alpha—spiritual—perspective, we see otherwise.

José Silva says that we prey *on* each other at beta. We pray *for* each other at alpha. It is a different kind of "praying."

In our experience, success, happiness, prosperity, and satisfaction come not from what we get, but from what we give. Keep in mind that you must have a balance: you give, and you also receive.

If you do not permit the people that you give to, to compensate you, you are cheating them of the wonderful opportunity to gain all of the benefits of giving. Be unselfish. Keep a balance in your life between giving and getting.

You are not the sole judge of the value of your problem solving efforts. You could be out there working very hard digging ditches, but if the ditches don't help anybody or solve any problems, then your work has no value.

You can determine the value of your work by the compensation that you receive.

It is not always a direct thing. When you do $5 worth of work for somebody, you may not receive $5 compensation from that person. But overall, you will be compensated.

A Real-Life Example

José Silva tells about a time when he healed a person in Nuevo Laredo, Mexico. One of his friends challenged him: "I'll bet they didn't even offer to reimburse you for the bridge tolls, did they?"

When the friend asked how much it had cost him to drive across the Rio Grande River into Mexico three times a day for a month to apply holistic faith healing techniques to the person, Mr. Silva said that with the cost of gasoline, bridge tolls, and time away from his work, it was probably $500.

"And you will never get it back," the friend said.

That night Mr. Silva didn't have any work to do, so his wife, Paula, asked if he would like to go with her to the bingo game at the church. Guess who won the grand prize that night?

That's right: José Silva.

Guess how much it was?

That's right: $500.

When he saw his friend the next day, he told him about it. "Maybe that's how higher intelligence compensated me for helping," Silva said.

"Oh, you and your silly ideas!" his skeptical friend replied.

The Principle That Led to José Silva's Method

Here are the final statements in our conditioning cycles. Mr. Silva put these statements at the end—the most powerful position—because of the value he feels they have.

You will continue to strive to take part in constructive and creative activities to make this a better world to live in, so that when we move on, we shall have left behind a better world for those who follow.

You will consider the whole of humanity, depending on their ages, as fathers or mothers, brothers or sisters, sons or daughters.

You are a superior human being; you have greater understanding, compassion, and patience with others.

Now that we have established a foundation to work from, it is time to learn how to find the alpha level and to use it to solve problems and manifest solutions in the physical world.

TWO

Using the Powerful
Alpha Brain Wave Level

We mentioned before that the alpha level is associated with a light level of sleep. This realization led José Silva to develop a simple, foolproof method that anyone can use to enter the alpha level and use it to get the information we need, make good decisions, create solutions, and implement those solutions.

People have claimed that Mr. Silva used hypnosis or other methods, but the truth is, he used classical conditioning.

With classical conditioning, you simply attach what you want to do to something that you already do naturally.

So if you want to learn to enter the alpha level with conscious awareness, let's hitch a ride as the body goes through the steps it is already familiar with when going to sleep:

- Find a comfortable position.
- Close your eyes.

- Relax physically.
- Relax mentally.

Do that, and your brain goes to alpha.

So why don't we fall asleep?

Because he gives us some simple things to do:

- Help your body to relax.
- Recall tranquil and passive scenes to help your mind relax.
- Repeat some beneficial statement.

To make it easier for you to enter the alpha level the next time, he associates the main steps with numbers, so that in the future all you need to do when you want to enter the alpha level with conscious awareness is to make yourself comfortable, close your eyes, and then:

- Mentally repeat and visualize the number 3 several times, and relax physically.
- Mentally repeat and visualize the number 2 several times, and relax mentally.
- Mentally repeat and visualize the number 1 several times, and take it for granted that you are at alpha.

The more you practice, the easier and faster it becomes until soon you can function at the alpha level, even with your eyes open, by simply desiring it.

The fastest and easiest way to learn is to have someone guide you in the beginning. To do this, choose one of the following methods:

- Go to the website SilvaESP.com/csv/ and stream or download a recording of the Long Relaxation Exercise, also known as the Silva Centering Exercise. (For the text, see appendix A of this book.)
- Be your own guide by recording the Silva conditioning cycles. The complete scripts are in the appendix. You can

follow the instructions and make your own recordings in your own voice. Or you can ask someone else to record it for you.

- If you are learning the Silva system along with someone else, you can take turns reading the exercise to teach other. They can watch you and pace themselves depending on how quickly you relax, and you can do the same for them.
- You can also memorize the steps and do them on your own. José Silva's brother Juan believed that it is better to do it yourself than to have somebody else guiding you.
- If you find yourself making an effort to recall the instructions, and therefore are not relaxing completely, then you can use the Morning Countdown system in appendix B.

José Silva recommended that when you learn on your own, you should accumulate a total of ten hours of practice with the Silva Centering Exercise in order to be confident of your ability to function at the alpha level.

Scientists thought it couldn't be done. Mr. Silva took several of his students into their lab to prove that it could. He had been doing it for years. He said it was the most valuable discovery he had made in his research: a way to use the subconscious consciously. But that is a contradiction in terms, he said, so he coined the term *inner conscious level.*

If you hear anybody else using that term, now you know where it came from.

All of our techniques are designed to work at the inner conscious level. Once you learn to reach that level, you will not need to go through the Centering Exercise to get there. With practice, you won't even need to close your eyes. You will be able to use the inner conscious level with your eyes open, as long as you don't focus and concentrate your eyesight on anything.

Eyesight Is like a Switch

You can "defocus" your vision and imagine being at alpha in order to function at the powerful alpha brain wave level, the ideal level of thinking and decision making.

Then simply focus your eyes to return to the faster beta brain wave frequencies, and use the beta level as you take action in the physical world.

Be Sure to Use the Genuine José Silva System

One more piece of advice:

Be careful about "Silva" products that have been changed or altered by somebody else after José Silva passed in 1999. There are a lot of them on the Internet. They have been altered by somebody who thinks their personal opinion is better than Mr. Silva's twenty-two years of scientific research.

He did make small changes from time to time. For instance: He used to have the phrase ". . . to take part in constructive and creative activities to make this a better world to live in," but some people didn't like ending a sentence with the word "in."

Many of us feel just as awkward with the phrase ". . . a better world in which to live."

So after thinking about it for a few seconds, he changed it to:

You will continue to strive to take part in constructive and creative activities to make the world a better place to live.

He had at least three dictionaries on his desk, both English and Spanish, and he used them to make sure that every word did the job he wanted it to do. The Silva systems never would have had the success they have enjoyed for more than half a century if he hadn't gotten it right.

How can you tell if you are getting the genuine José Silva coursework? The resources throughout this book only offer genuine José Silva products that have not been changed or altered by anyone else after his passing. José Silva Jr. makes sure of that.

THREE

Sleep Control, To Awake Control, and Awake Control

Have you ever had one of those nights when it is really hard for you to get to sleep?

Maybe you had a big day: something wonderful happened to you, and you are still excited about it.

Or maybe you have a big day coming up tomorrow, and you are excited about your opportunities.

At any rate, you need a good night's sleep so that you will be fresh tomorrow to take advantage of the opportunities that await you. You need to manage your energies.

You don't want to be like the little girl who told her daddy: "Mother sure doesn't know much about little girls."

"Why is that?" he asked.

"Because she makes me go to bed when I'm not sleepy and makes me get up when I am!"

Sometimes what keeps people awake is their problems.

They worry about the problems they faced during the day and about whether they solved them correctly.

They worry about the problems they have to deal with tomorrow.

All of that worry makes it difficult to go to sleep.

The same thing makes it difficult to get up in the morning, because it is time for them to deal with those problems.

Later, you will learn techniques to help you deal with the problems. We all have problems to solve. That's part of life.

When you do not have any way to deal with problems, it's very stressful and frustrating.

When you have a way to deal with them, they become projects.

For now, we are going to learn a formula-type technique for self-management. It will help you to get a good night's sleep every night, so that you will be fresh and ready to deal with the problems and the opportunities of each and every day.

This technique is so boring that we guarantee it will put you to sleep. Quickly.

When you feel tired and run down, stressed out, and you are not as alert as you should be, you limit your options. It is more difficult for you to make good decisions and choose the correct options that will bring you more success.

Some people are so tired and frustrated that the best they can do is hope that they don't make too many mistakes during the day. If you want to choose success, you will be much better off with an attitude that you are going to take advantage of the opportunities that the day offers you and do something great.

Some people take sleeping pills to get to sleep at night and then take amphetamines to wake up in the morning. Or they drink themselves into an alcoholic stupor at night and fill their system with caffeine (coffee) in the morning.

This is not good for you. Every time you use drugs, any drugs, they cause side effects. Sometimes the side effects are worse than the condition you are trying to cure.

So we try to stay away from drugs as much as we can. The Silva Sleep Control Technique will take care of that problem.

In this chapter, we'll explain three formula-type techniques for your benefit. The formulas are in appendix C.

These formulas will help you get to sleep naturally, without drugs, to wake up without clocks, and to be refreshed and awake when necessary, such as when driving late at night.

These are actual formulas. They are like recipes. Follow them exactly. José Silva invested twenty-two years working out the exact wording. He worked with thousands of people. Use them exactly as written. After you have had success with them, if you want to experiment with changing them, you can do so.

If you have questions about a technique, read the formula and pay attention to the words that José Silva used. He was very careful in his choice of words. Do what he did, and look them up in the dictionary to help you understand their exact meaning.

When you are first learning be sure to use our standard method of entering level—not some other kind of meditation. If you use some other means of entering level, we do not know what level you are at, so we do not know what kind of results to expect.

If you have practiced the Centering Exercise several times, then you can shorten the procedure.

Enter Level Faster and Easier

Instead of going through all of the physical and mental relaxation, just find a comfortable position, relax, take a deep breath, and while exhaling, mentally repeat and visualize the number 3 several times, and relax physically.

Then take another deep breath, and while exhaling, mentally repeat and visualize the number 2 several times, and relax mentally.

Then take another deep breath, and while exhaling, mentally repeat and visualize the number 1 several times, and recall the feeling of being at alpha.

Then you can deepen yourself if you wish by doing a 10-to-1 countdown, relaxing your eyelids, or projecting yourself mentally to your ideal place of relaxation. You can also repeat some beneficial statements.

Then you can apply the formulas. All of the formulas are in appendix C for your convenience. Before we get to them, let's talk about sleep, and how you can get a good night's sleep—natural, physiologic sleep, without drugs.

The Sleep Construct

When you sleep at night, your brain cycles through all different frequencies, from the alpha frequencies of light sleep and dreaming through the deep theta frequencies and all the way to the very low delta frequencies of deepest sleep. These sleep and dream cycles last about 90 minutes each.

The first cycle of natural sleep goes to the very low delta brain wave frequencies, and you spend most of the 90 minutes there. Then the brain frequency increase to about 7 cycles per second, the top of the alpha frequency range, and you have a short dream.

In the second 90-minute sleep-and-dream cycle, you do not go to as low a frequency: you spend less time in delta and more time in alpha. That pattern continues with the following sleep-and-dream cycles.

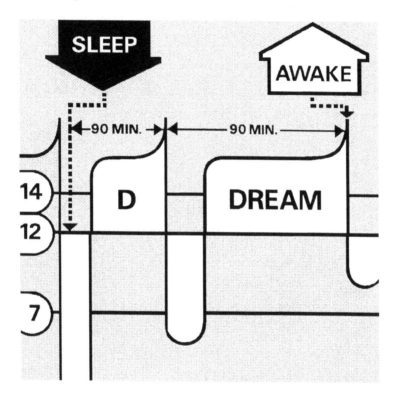

Sleep deprivation studies have shown that it is important that you spend sufficient time at the alpha level during sleep. When you are deprived of alpha sleep, there are serious side effects, such as irritability, loss of ability to learn and to recall information, and sometimes even mild hallucinations.

Sleeping pills and alcohol tend to take you past alpha into the lower theta brain wave frequencies and deprive you of much-needed alpha sleep. Learning and using this technique will help you get the alpha sleep your body needs.

Now here's how to use the Silva Sleep Control Technique:

Sleep Control

Whenever you are ready to go to sleep, enter your level, and apply the sleep control technique.

First, visualize a chalkboard. (By *visualize*, I mean to recall a chalkboard that you have seen before.) Then imagine that you are standing at the chalkboard with chalk in one hand and an eraser in the other.

You will then mentally draw a large circle on the chalkboard. Then mentally draw a big X within the circle. You will then proceed to erase the X from within the circle, starting at the center and erasing towards the inner edges of the circle, being careful not to erase the circle in the least.

Once you erase the X from within the circle, to the right and outside of the circle write the word *deeper*. Every time you write the word *deeper*, you will enter a deeper, healthier level of mind, in the direction of normal, natural, healthy sleep.

Then write a big number 100 within the circle. Proceed to erase the number 100, being careful not to erase the circle in the least. Then, to the right and outside of the circle, go over the word *deeper*.

Then write a big number 99 in the circle. Erase it, and go over the word *deeper*. Then write the numbers 98, 97, 96, and so on until you fall asleep.

Preprogram the Technique to Work for You

You know that in order to use a computer, you need to first install a program into it. That is, you turn on the computer and install a set of instructions.

Then, when you want to use the computer, you turn it on, call up the program that has been installed, and use it.

Your brain is a computer, so in order to use the formula-type techniques most effectively, you first "install" the program in your brain.

To do that, simply enter your level, and go through the steps in the technique. You can record the formula and play it back for yourself. Or you can get the audio version of this book at SilvaESP.com. As an owner of this book, you can get it at a discount by submitting the coupon code SuccessBook when you check out.

To Awake Control

The next formula is To Awake Control to learn to wake up without an alarm clock.

This is more than a self-management technique; it is also a communications technique.

It establishes a type of communication between your mind, your brain, and your body.

What you are actually learning to do, is to use your mind to help you do the right thing at the right time.

At the alpha level, you can give instructions to your mind to cause an effect in your body. You instruct your mind to awaken your body at a specific time.

Here is how you apply this technique:

At night, when you are in bed ready to go to sleep, enter your level with the 3 to 1 Method. Once you are at your level, visualize (recall) a clock. Mentally reset the time on the clock to indicate the time that you want to awaken, and tell yourself mentally, "This is the time I want to awaken, and this is the time I am going to awaken."

Remain at your level, and go to sleep from level.

You will awaken at your desired time, feeling fine and in perfect health.

How Your Mind Influences Your Body

Who keeps time? Your mind, which is not physical and therefore never needs to sleep, keeps time for you.

How does your mind wake you up? Sometimes you might awaken thinking that a barking dog or a car horn awakened you. This is the way your mind uses imagination to get your attention. Or you might awaken without realizing why.

We are not concerned with how you get up in the morning. Our real goal is for you to develop your ability to use your mind, to build a foundation that will be valuable to you later as you learn additional techniques.

By practicing this technique, you will develop your "Mind Control" ability and will function better with the ESP techniques that you learn in the Silva ESP training, especially those that involve mind-to-mind communication.

Mr. Silva recommends that the best time to practice the To Awake Control technique to get it to work for you is when you are not under a lot of pressure. You need to have confidence in the technique. So program yourself to wake up on a morning when you will not miss anything important (like getting to work on time) if you oversleep.

You can still build up your desire by entering your level and thinking of all the reasons you have for getting this technique to work for you. Make sure you have a strong desire, and the technique will work for you.

Once you learn how to use your mind, which never sleeps, to wake up your body at the time you desire, imagine all of the many ways that you can use your mind to help you do the right thing at the right time.

If you have a young child, you can program yourself to always remember to check the back seat before you lock your car to make sure you are not leaving your child behind.

You can program to remember important anniversaries and birthdays.

You can program to remember important business meetings and deadlines.

How to Be More Alert Instantly

The third formula is Awake Control, for remaining awake longer.

This technique is designed for use any time you are drowsy or sleepy or feel low on energy. This could happen if you are driving home late at night, for instance.

There are five steps involved. These five steps are found in one form or another in the other Silva techniques. Each step is important; if you leave one out, there is a good chance that the technique will not work as planned.

Here are the five steps:

1. Recognize the existing situation.
2. Establish your goal.
3. Make a plan for reaching your goal.
4. Apply the method that you planned to use.
5. Take it for granted that you have succeeded.

Awake Control Formula

Whenever you feel drowsy and sleepy and you don't want to feel drowsy and sleepy, especially when you are driving, pull to the side of the road, stop your motor, and enter level with the 3 to 1 Method.

At level, mentally tell yourself, "I am drowsy and sleepy; I don't want to be drowsy and sleepy; I want to be wide awake, feeling fine, and in perfect health."

Then tell yourself mentally, "I am going to count from 1 to 5. At the count of 5, I will open my eyes, be wide awake, feeling fine and in perfect health. I will not be drowsy and sleepy; I will be wide awake."

Count mentally, slowly: 1, 2, 3; at the count of 3, mentally remind yourself that at the count of 5, "I will open my eyes, be wide awake, feeling fine and in perfect health."

Then mentally count slowly to 4, then 5; at the count of 5 and with your eyes open, tell yourself mentally, "I am wide awake, feeling fine, and in perfect health, feeling better than before."

Remember, it is important to take it for granted that you will feel refreshed.

After you have applied the formula, assume it has worked. Act as if it has worked. Pretend it has worked. Even if it doesn't feel as if it has worked, pretend that it does feel as if it has worked. Tell yourself a little fib, and pretend that you feel wide awake and in perfect health, and you will in fact feel wide awake and in perfect health.

Make up your mind that you are going to make it happen, and your mind will make it happen.

You can easily adapt this formula for other needs. If you are tired and exhausted, for instance, just change the wording from "drowsy and sleepy" to "tired and exhausted." If you feel nervous and intimidated when talking to important people, use the same approach to correct that problem.

What other kind of problem would you like to correct with this programming technique? Perhaps you want to feel more confident in a certain kind of situation.

If that's the case, then follow the same five steps. At your level, tell yourself mentally that in a certain kind of situation, you do not feel confident. Tell yourself that you want to feel confident and self-assured. Then tell yourself that whenever you find yourself in this situation, you will take a deep breath, and as you exhale, you will relax and act in a confident manner. That's the first three steps: the problem, the solution, and a plan.

The next time you find yourself in that situation, work your plan: take a deep breath, relax, and act as if you are already a confident, self-assured person.

It will be best to program just prior to the event. You can also incorporate other techniques that you will learn later in this course to help you succeed:

- The Three Fingers Technique
- Visualization, imagination, and the Mirror of the Mind

All of these techniques will help you take more control of your life, so that you will have more choices—so that you will be able to choose success whenever you desire.

When you are ready to "install" these programs in your brain, use your preferred method to enter your level and program these techniques. The formulas are in appendix C.

Note: If you want to review any of the information about any of these three techniques, then please do so before you enter your level and impress and program the formulas. Here's why:

When you impress and program these formulas at your level, it is like planting a seed. You do not want to dig that seed up right away, but want to give it a chance to sprout and begin to grow.

Therefore you do not want to go back and study this technique any more until after you have slept on it. Once you have gone through at least one sleep-and-dream cycle, then you can review it as much as you like.

You can go ahead and use the techniques tonight. That's fine. We just don't want to analyze them right after programming them. Just move on to a new project, the next techniques, or whatever else you have to do today.

For a free video demonstrating the Sleep Control technique go to the web page SilvaESP.com/csv/ and use the voucher CSV22 for instant access.

FOUR

Programmed Dreams and Headache Control

Dreams are like postcards from your subconscious. They can give you a lot of information about yourself, about how you think and about the things you like and dislike.

Some people have said that the greatest benefit they got from the Silva course was what they learned about themselves by remembering and understanding their dreams.

There was a young woman who took the course with us to help her pass the bar exam. She had graduated from law school but was having trouble with the bar exam that she had to pass in order to begin practicing law.

The memory and test taking techniques that you will learn a little later didn't help her. She knew the information, but she just couldn't seem to get it right when taking the exam.

Then she programmed to have a dream. In her programmed dream, she dreamed about the fact that she was adopted. That was something she almost never thought about: she and her adoptive parents have so much love for each other that she usually thinks of them as her natural parents.

When she went to her level to analyze the dream and figure out what it meant, she began to recall the feelings she'd had long ago about not being wanted by her natural parents, being "thrown away," abandoned.

Maybe it was those old feelings of unworthiness, she thought, of not being loved, of not being lovable—maybe those feelings were still buried deep inside. Maybe she was somebody who wasn't worthy of good things or accomplishing big goals.

At her level, she canceled out those feelings and told herself—at a deep level—that it was not her fault that her parents put her up for adoption. She reminded herself how much she was loved and appreciated by her adoptive parents.

This all made her feel much better. More importantly, she passed the bar exam without any trouble this time.

José Silva says that there is no such thing as a problem without a solution, just problems for which we do not yet have enough information to know what the solution is.

This lady obtained information in her programmed dream that helped her solve her problem and reach her goal.

A Skeptical Real Estate Developer

Here's a story of someone who found a solution to another kind of problem.

A man, whom I'll call Tom, attended the Silva course with us in Albuquerque, New Mexico. Tom had a fabulous experience with the Dream Control Technique that probably saved him tens of thousands of dollars.

Tom was a very successful developer and had put together many projects over the last twenty or thirty years. He had earned a lot of money by developing housing projects, subdivisions, and commercial properties.

Tom was a bit skeptical when he attended our free introductory lecture. Actually, he wasn't sure he should trust us at all. So I made a deal with him.

I told him to come on Saturday morning and give me a check. I told him that I'd put it in my pocket, and he could keep his eye on me and his check. I pointed out that I wouldn't even have a chance to deposit his check until Monday. I said I wouldn't deposit it until he told me to.

I assured him that if he wanted his check back at any time, I'd give it to him. He was free to leave if he wanted to—with his check in hand.

I also told him that at the end of the weekend, he could take his money back and that would be that, or he could tell me to hold it and he'd come back the next weekend and see how that went, or he could tell me to deposit the check. Whatever he wanted.

That satisfied him, and he decided to try out the course.

He was really glad that he did.

After that first weekend, he told me to hold on to the check and that he would be back the next weekend to see how the second half of the course went.

When he returned for the second half of the course, he had a wonderful story to tell us:

He had decided to use Dream Control. He knew that he dreamed every night, but he had never bothered to analyze his dreams or see if they contained any useful information. But he had a business situation that he was uncomfortable with, so he went straight to Dream Control Step 3 to program a dream to give him information that he could use to help him make the right decision.

The problem that he had in mind was whether to accept a business proposal that had been offered to him. It all sounded good, he said, almost too good, and something seemed to be holding him back.

That night he dreamed about an old childhood friend, whom he hadn't seen in thirty years. He wondered why he had dreamed of his friend; it didn't seem to have anything to do with his current situation. "I hadn't thought about that person in the last twenty-five years," Tom told the class.

Tom went to his level and thought about it: He and his friend had lived near each other, they had grown up together, gone to school together, and . . . oh, that's right . . . they had gone into business together after college.

And it didn't go well.

Tom didn't give us details, but said that the business arrangement cost him a lot of money and also cost him his friendship.

As Tom thought back on his experiences with his former friend, he began to recall some of the details of their business dealings.

Suddenly he realized that there were many similarities between the business transactions of thirty years before and the current proposal.

"It didn't cause me to call off the deal," Tom told us, "but now I have a list of questions to ask and several things to check out and make sure of before I decide to proceed."

Tom said that doing this could potentially save him a great deal of money.

Then he told me to go ahead and deposit the check. He had gotten his money's worth and a whole lot more just by finding an additional way to draw on his past experiences to help him make better business decisions today.

Everybody Dreams

Some people say that they don't have dreams, but scientists assure us that we all have dreams, although we may not remember them.

Dreams are communications tools to help you get information and make decisions.

You can use the information from dreams to help you manage your life better, as the attorney did.

You can also use the information in dreams to guide you in your programming, using the techniques that you are learning in José Silva's Choose Success Master Course.

Dreams can provide various kinds of information. It can provide information that is stored on in your memory banks, as in the two examples we have just seen.

Dreams can go way beyond that. Your mind can bring you information from anywhere that information happens to be.

- Other people's brain cells—their memory banks.
- From higher intelligence on the other side.
- From anywhere that information is stored.

There is evidence that records of everything that has ever happened on this planet are stored somewhere. People have given various names to this: universal mind, the akashic records, and so on.

Your mind never sleeps. So if you give it instructions to find information that you can use to solve a problem, it will do so.

We're telling you this and including it in the course because it's a very natural phenomenon. Many people do it.

Have you ever had a precognitive dream? That is, you dreamed about something, and the next day, or a few days later, it happened. Many people have.

Have you ever had a dream that contained information that helped you understand a situation or helped you solve a problem? Many people have.

In fact, when we ask this question of people who attend our free introductory lectures—people who have not been through the Silva training—as many as two-thirds of those people will answer "Yes" to at least one of those questions. It seems to be a very common experience.

Dream Telepathy

There is a lot of evidence for mind-to-mind communication in dreams. There is a fascinating book titled *Dream Telepathy* by a researcher named Stanley Krippner, a specialist in this area. He proved that mental projection exists.

Here's how he did it:

In a sleep and dream laboratory, there was a subject in one room who was wired up with monitoring equipment and then told to go to sleep.

In another room was another subject. When the first subject was asleep and dreaming, this second subject was told to open the drawer, select one envelope at random, open it, and then concentrate on the picture in it, thinking of the sleeping individual.

Then the researchers woke the first subject up and asked him to tell about his dream.

Later they gave the reports of the dreams and the pictures that had been transmitted mentally to a third person, and asked them if any of the pictures matched any of the dreams.

They were able to match up a large number of pictures with the correct dreams.

Researchers have learned when to wake a person up so that they can remember their dreams.

If they awaken you at the beginning of the dream cycle, you remember nothing.

If they awaken you halfway, it is a confused dream. You don't know what to make of it. It is like opening a book in the middle.

When they awaken you at the end of the dream cycle, you will remember your dreams.

With the Silva Dream Control Technique you will program yourself to wake up at the right time to remember your dreams.

You can easily learn to control your dreams. If you are having bad dreams, just program at your level that you are having bad dreams, you don't want to have bad dreams, you want to have good dreams, and from now on, you are going to have only good dreams.

Destroying Monsters

It is human nature to fear whatever is new. The subjective (mental) dimension is a new frontier for us to explore. The science of psychorientology is just beginning to map this new territory. We have been at it only since 1944!

Sometimes people encounter experiences that they do not understand, and the fight-or-flight response kicks in.

Psychorientology research is helping us to understand what is going on, so that we can use this dimension to help us correct more problems and manifest more solutions.

Here is a problem that José and Paula Silva ran into one night:

They were visiting Monterrey, Mexico, and left their children with a baby sitter in the hotel while they went out for the evening.

The baby sitter wanted to watch television, so she told the children to stay in bed or the bogeyman would get them. As she told them this, she tapped her hand against the wall and told the children, "Hear that? That's the monster, and he will get you if you get out of bed!"

The children stayed in bed.

While this may have solved the baby sitter's problem, it also created a problem for the children. Now they were afraid to get out of the bed after dark to go to the bathroom, or to get a drink of water.

It did no good for their father to assure them that there was no such thing as a bogeyman. They knew better: at night, they could "see" the bogeyman . . . in their imagination. "But that's not real," their father tried to convince them. "It is your imagination." They were not convinced.

Then he had an idea to remedy the situation. "The next time you see the bogeyman," he told them, "you point your finger at him and shake your finger at him as hard as you can. Every time you shake your finger, that monster will get smaller and smaller and smaller," he said.

The youngsters started shaking their fingers rapidly, until they had shrunk the monsters down to a very small size, so small that they could hold the monsters in their hands.

After that, there was no more problem with the bogeyman.

"People sometimes let their imagination get the best of them," Mr. Silva said. "They imagine things so vividly that they paralyze themselves; they are afraid to take action, because of the monsters they have created with their imagination.

"It is like a psychosomatic illness," he explained. "If you fear something enough, you can bring about the very condition that you fear. It is as Job said in the Bible: 'That which I feared the most has come upon me.' But you are doing it to yourself; nobody else is. The good news is that you have the power to change it simply by changing your mind. Make up your mind to change, and use our techniques, and you will change."

You make the changes, just as you learned in the last chapter: at your level, acknowledge the problem, state your goal, outline your plan, take action, and claim your end result. You can do this to eliminate nightmares, slay monsters, or change anything that you want to change.

Dream Control Formula

You learn Dream Control in three steps:

Dream Control step 1. To practice remembering a dream, you will enter level 1 with the 3 to 1 Method. Once at level 1, you will mentally tell yourself, "I want to remember a dream, and I am going to remember a dream." You will then go to sleep from level 1.

You will awaken during the night or in the morning with a vivid recollection of a dream. Have a paper and pencil ready to write it down.

When you are satisfied that Dream Control step 1 is responding, then start with Dream Control step 2.

Dream Control step 2. To practice remembering dreams, you will enter level 1 with the 3 to 1 Method. Once at level 1, mentally tell yourself, "I want to remember my dreams, and I am going to remember my dreams." You will then go to sleep from level 1.

You will awaken several times during the night and in the morning with vivid recollections of dreams. Have a paper and pencil ready to write them down. When you are satisfied that Dream Control step 2 is responding, then start with Dream Control step 3.

Dream Control step 3. To practice generating a dream that you can remember, understand, and use for problem solving, you will enter level 1 with the 3 to 1 Method. Once at level 1, mentally tell yourself, "I want to have a dream that will contain information to solve the problem I have in mind." State the problem and add, "I will have such a dream, remember it, and understand it." You will then go to sleep from level 1.

You may awaken during the night with a vivid recollection of the desired dream, or you may awaken in the morning with a vivid recollection of such a dream. You will have this dream, remember it, and understand it.

Headache Relief

Headache Control follows the same general format as the Awake Control technique, which you learned in the previously. Here are the steps:

1. Identify the problem.
2. State your goal.
3. Make a plan.

4. Work your plan.

5. Claim your reward.

Here's how it goes:

If you have a tension-type headache, enter level 1 with the 3 to 1 Method. Once at level 1, mentally tell yourself, "I have a headache; I feel a headache; I don't want to have a headache; I don't want to feel a headache.

"I am going to count from 1 to 5, and at the count of 5, I will open my eyes, be wide awake, feeling fine and in perfect health. I will then have no headache. I will then feel no headache."

You will then count slowly from 1 to 2, then to 3, and at the count of 3, you will remind yourself mentally that, "At the count of 5, I will open my eyes, be wide awake, feeling fine and in perfect health; I will then have no discomfort in my head; I will then feel no discomfort in my head."

Notice that we have made a change at level 3, from "ache" to "discomfort." We left the ache behind. You will then proceed to mentally count slowly to 4, then to 5, and at the count of 5, and with your eyes open, you will say to yourself mentally, "I am wide awake, feeling fine and in perfect health. I have no discomfort in my head. I feel no discomfort in my head. And this is so."

If you have a migraine headache go through the same procedure, but use three applications five minutes apart.

Enter level 1 with the 3 to 1 Method. Once at level 1, go through the same procedure as in the tension-type headache application, but use three applications five minutes apart.

You will note that the first application will have reduced the discomfort by a certain amount. Wait five minutes, then apply the second application. The second application will take care of a greater amount of the discomfort. Wait five more minutes, and apply the third application. With the third application, all of the discomfort will have disappeared.

From then on, when symptoms appear, one application will take care of the migraine problem. As you continue to take care of this problem in this manner, the symptoms will appear less frequently, until the body forgets how to cause them, bringing to an end the migraine problem without the use of drugs. And this is so.

To correct health problems, controls are applied under a doctor's supervision.

Remember, this is not a cure for a medical condition. It is to relieve tension-type headaches.

If your headache is caused by tension, this will take care of the cause of the problem.

If the headaches keep coming back, you may have a medical problem. Be sure to consult your doctor. There are techniques in other Silva courses for dealing with serious health problems. You can also use the techniques in this course, such as the Mirror of the Mind, which we will cover a little later, to help your doctor help your body heal itself.

A cautionary note here: whenever you are working on health problems, work under a doctor's supervision. This is not a substitute for competent medical care, but a supplement to it.

And remember the value of spending fifteen minutes at level every day. If you have a serious health problem, go to level for fifteen minutes three times a day.

FIVE

The Mental Screen and Memory Pegs

When you have a problem and you want to correct it mentally, you need to transfer it from the objective dimension—the physical dimension—to the subjective, the mental, dimension.

You also need to use the correct language.

The language of the brain, the language of the mind and the subjective dimension, is not English or Spanish or German. It is visual.

Everybody understands pictures. Your brain understands pictures. It may not understand every spoken language in the world, but it does understand pictures. Your mind also understands pictures.

The universal language that is understood by everybody everywhere, the language that is understood in all dimensions, is visual.

The Mental Screen, which you will learn about next, is a communications tool.

The Mental Screen allows you to transfer problems from the objective dimension to the subjective dimension so that you can correct them.

The Mental Screen is also the means by which you can communicate in the subjective dimension.

- You can communicate with other people, with their minds and their brains.
- You can communicate in this manner with higher intelligence, with your helpers on the other side.
- You can also get information from wherever that information is stored.

Before we go any further, let's define some terms, so that we are all talking about the same thing:

1. The word *see*. You *see* with your eyes. That is the only way to see anything—with your eyes. Whenever you focus your eyes or even attempt to focus your eyes, your brain goes to 20 cycles per second beta brain frequency. You can use any of your other senses at alpha, but the sense of sight requires your brain to be at beta.

2. The word *visualize*. You *visualize* with your mind. *To visualize* means that you remember what something looks like. In order to remember something, you have to have seen it or imagined it before. Visualization is memory: the memory of what something looks like.

3. The word *imagine*. To *imagine* means to think about what something looks like that you have never experienced before, something you have not seen before, have not imagined before. It is a creative process, because what you

are thinking about is something you have never seen or imagined before.

Visualization is *not* like seeing. It is not even like dreaming. It is like remembering. It is remembering what something looks like.

Let's take an example that uses *seeing, visualization,* and *imagination.*

Do you remember *seeing,* on television or in a movie, the dog Lassie? If not, then recall any dog that you have seen. Do you remember what the dog looked like?

- What size was this dog?
- How big?
- How long was its hair?
- What color was it?
- What did its tail look like?
- Its ears?

Remembering what you have seen before is *visualization.* You have just visualized a dog that you have seen previously.

How many legs did the dog have? Four? Now can you imagine what the dog would look like if it had six legs? Where would the other two legs be? At the front? The back? In the middle? Where would they be? Imagine what that would look like.

Now you have just used *imagination* to create a mental picture of something that you have never seen or imagined before.

It is very simple. You can do it with your eyes open or closed. You can do it at beta or at alpha.

In order to imagine things and have them manifest in the physical world, your visualization and imagination must be at alpha.

For now, it is easiest for you to do this with your eyes closed, because you shut out distractions. Later, with practice, you can learn how to function at alpha with your eyes open and defocused.

If you go back and recall that dog that you imagined with six legs, and recall what the dog looks like, and where the two extra legs are—the front, the back, or the middle   you are visualizing, because you are recalling what something looks like that you imagined previously.

A few people have very vivid mental images when they do this. Most people have some kind of mental image. Some of us simply know what the dog would look like. That's the way I function. You might say that I imagine what the mental image would look like.

The good news is, that's all that is required to be successful in functioning in the subjective dimension.

You want to get accustomed to thinking about what things look like. Some people use words to think things through; others use feelings. These are all good, and are important. It is also important, especially for mental functioning in the subjective dimension to think visually as well. So you want to get used to thinking visually, so that you will visualize and imagine what things look like.

This is very important when you use a programming technique like the Mirror of the Mind, which you will learn a little later. It is important because you must first visualize the problem that you desire to correct, and then you must imagine the problem corrected; you must imagine your goal.

How to Develop a Picture-Perfect Memory

How would you like a technique to help you develop and improve your ability to visualize and imagine on your Mental Screen? We have a technique to do that. As an added bonus, this same technique will also help to improve your memory. What a bargain—two benefits for the price of one!

First, let's define the Mental Screen and show you how to locate it.

Your Mental Screen can be like a surround movie screen or a giant 360-degree computer screen.

Your Mental Screen will be upwards and about thirty feet (about nine meters) away from you like the screen you see when you are in a theater. You can project and detect images on the screen behind you or off to the sides if you need to.

You want your Mental Screen to be above the horizontal plane of sight. You want to physically turn your eyes up slightly. Not so much that you are uncomfortable, but definitely upwards. This helps to produce more alpha rhythm in the brain. Nobody knows why for sure, but it does. It will help you to stay on alpha while you are using your visualization and imagination to correct problems and reach your goals.

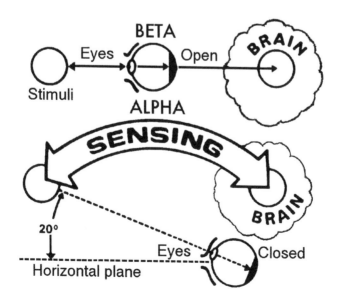

To locate your Mental Screen, begin with your eyes closed, turned slightly upward from the horizontal plane of sight, at an angle of approximately 20 degrees.

The area that you perceive with your mind is your Mental Screen.

Without using your eyelids as screens, sense your Mental Screen to be out, away from your body.

To improve the use of your Mental Screen, project images or mental pictures onto the screen, especially images having color. Concentrate on mentally sensing and visualizing true color.

Do this with your eyes closed and turned slightly upward, and imagine the screen to be out and away from you. This is where you are going to detect and project mental images when you use visualization and imagination.

The Mental Screen is to transfer from one dimension to the other, from one aspect to the other, where you are receiving or transmitting. It shows on your Mental Screen.

So to transmit something, you project it onto your Mental Screen. To detect it, you sense it on your Mental Screen.

To help you improve the use of your Mental Screen, which will help you to visualize and imagine better, we'll learn a portion of a memory course.

Mr. Silva got this memory peg system from a course by Bruno Furst. If you want to know more, you can check his books, or those of a more recent practitioner like Harry Lorayne, who uses the same system.

With this system, we convert numbers to letters—to consonants—and then use the letters to form the names of objects that we can remember and use as our pegs.

The pegs never change. Only the list of things to remember changes.

And since our number system is a decimal system, once we learn the first ten pegs—the ones that represent the numbers 1, 2, 3, 4, 5, 6, 7, 8, 9, and 0—then we can make any other number out of those.

So the numbers represent letters, and letters numbers.

Using visualization, imagination, association, and exaggeration makes it easier to remember things.

We tend to remember things that we associate with having a good time. Most people can remember Christmas presents they got as children, or great birthday presents, or special events like their first date or their senior prom.

We'll show you how this works by showing you how to remember a list of objects. We'll just use ten objects, but you can remember many more if you know how.

Here's how:

1. You get a good mental image of the object to remember.
2. You associate the object that you want to remember with something you already know, in a memorable way. This is like having a "peg" to hang your "picture" on.

For now, I'll provide the pegs for you to hang your mental pictures on. Later I'll show you how to remember the pegs so that you can have as many lists of items in your memory as you desire.

For a free video demonstrating the Memory Peg system go to the web page SilvaESP.com/csv/ and use the voucher CSV22 for instant access.

Practice Session

Let's pick some items to remember:

1. Object: *book*. Peg word: *Tea*.

    Mental picture: *José Silva's Choose Success Master Course* book in a glass of iced *Tea*. Exaggerate it in size or color or amount, make it something you would be sure to remember if you saw it in real life.

2. Object: *car*. Peg word: *Noah*.

    Mental picture: Red convertible, sports model, spouse in front with you, kids in back seat, going up the gangplank onto *Noah*'s Ark.

3. Object: *vacation*. Peg word: *May*.

    Mental picture: Sunny island in the Pacific. Sitting under shade of palm tree, drinking cool coconut drink, pictured on the calendar month of *May*.

4. Object: *money*. Peg word: *Ray*.

    Mental picture: Stack of $100 bills with *Rays* of light lighting them up.

5. Object: *house*. Peg word: *Law*.

    Mental picture: Red roof, white brick, two-story house. *Law* enforcement officer guarding the house, stopping people from coming in.

6. Object: TV. Peg word: *Jaw*.

    Mental picture: projection screen, 60 inch picture, surround sound. Man with large *Jaw* balancing it on his *Jaw*, or eating it

7. Object: *motorcycle*. Peg word: *Key*.

Mental picture: Harley-Davidson. Big hog. White and maroon. *Key* winds it up.

8. Object: *cowboy boots*. Peg word: *Fee*.

Mental picture: Black rattlesnake skin boots with a *Fee*: a price tag of $8 million.

9. Object: *diamond ring*. Peg word: *Bay* (land and water).

Mental picture: Very large gemstone, gold band, pearls around stone, floating in a *Bay* filled with diamond rings.

10. Object: *computer*. Peg word: *ToeS*.

Mental picture: Computer. Gigabyte of storage, tower system, all the trimmings, big color monitor, working the mouse with your ten *ToeS*.

See how easy it is to remember a list of objects when you associate them with something familiar and make them memorable?

How to Remember the Peg Words

So how do you remember the pegs?

This system is designed to make it as easy as possible to remember the first ten pegs.

For instance, to convert the number 1 to a consonant, just put a *top* on the number 1, and you have a T.

The consonants that we use are based on the phonetic sound. That is, if your teeth, tongue, and lips are in the same position, it has the same value. Like the letters T and D. Say those out loud, and you will see that your tongue is in the same position both times, as are your lips. B and P are the same.

Vowels have no value. Only consonants have value. Vowels are used to fill in and make words. Similarly, the W, H, and Y have no value, but are used for fill in to make words.

So, if the number 1 is always a T or a D, let's start with the T and use our vowels to make a word: A, E, I, O, and U. The E works fine there: *tea*.

If you take the number 2 and lay it on its side, it resembles the letter N.

Turn the number 3 on its side, and it looks like an M.

Give the number 4 a crutch, and it resembles an R.

The number 5 is represented by the consonant L. One way to help you remember that is the Roman Numeral L, which starts with a 5—it is the number 50.

Open up the number 6, turn it around, and you get a J.

The number 7 is tired, so it turns around and leans against the wall: K.

Number 8 has two loops, like the cursive F.

Turn the number 9 over, and you have a lower case b.

The final digit is 0, so let's twist it open for an S.

For numbers 10 and larger, simply combine the letters of the corresponding numerals. For example, 10 is T (1) combined with S (0). The peg words are *ToeS* or *ToyS*.

Here are the first thirty peg words, with alternates:

1. Tea, Tie
2. Noah, kNee (the k is silent)
3. May, Ma
4. Ray, Rye
5. Law, ell

6. Jaw, SHoe ("j" and "sh" sound similar)

7. Key, Cow (hard "c" sounds like "k")

8. Fee, ivy (sound similar)

9. Bay, Bee

10. ToeS, ToyS

11. ToT, TooT

12. TiN, ToN

13. TaM, ToMb (b is silent)

14. TaR, TiRe

15. TaiL, ToweL

16. Tissue, dish (sound similar)

17. TacK, TuG

18. Taffy, doVe

19. TuB, ToP

20. NoSe, NooSe

21. NeT, kNot

22. NuN, NooN

23. NaMe, gNoMe (g is silent)

24. NeRo, NoRway

25. NaiL, NiL

26. Niche, Notch (sound similar)

27. NecK, NaG

28. kNiFE, NaVY (sound similar)

29. kNoB (k is silent), NaP

30. Moss, Mice

Your brain has the capacity to remember a great deal. Scientists say that the human brain is the most highly structured and complex object in the universe. You'll be amazed at what it is capable of—at what *you* are capable of.

Enhance Your Genius Faculties

When you improve the use of the Mental Screen with visualization, it helps to enhance your imagination, memory, and clairvoyance. Our goal is clairvoyance.

The individuals who put this system together found a solution to memory work.

Our objective is not to give you a memory course but to give you something to work with that is used in memory courses to enhance the use of your Mental Screen to make it easier for you to become clairvoyant.

Memory experts don't know what it is to become clairvoyant. Their field is to get you to improve your memory. Our field is to get you to improve your clairvoyance. It is part of our system, because it has to do with mental pictures

If you really want to choose success, you will practice the memory pegs. We are putting in your hands the power to choose success.

You can choose to practice the memory pegs or not. It is up to you. But if you want to improve your communications skills in the subjective dimension—the mental dimension—you will choose to learn and practice the memory pegs.

SIX

The Three Fingers Technique, Speed Learning, and Test Taking

How would you like a technique that will produce alpha functioning instantly, at any time, even with your eyes open?

How would you like to have a technique that you can use to help you say the right thing at the right time? Imagine how that would help you to attain successful results more frequently.

You can learn to do all that and more with the Silva Three Fingers Technique.

The Three Fingers Technique is a trigger mechanism that reminds you of something that you have programmed before.

For instance, you can program yourself to use the Three Fingers Technique to help you relax in tense situations. You already know the steps to use:

- First, enter your level and state the problem: *I get nervous when talking to my boss.*
- Next, your goal: *I want to remain relaxed and confident.*

- Third, make a plan: *Whenever I am talking to my boss and I feel tense and nervous, I will bring together the tips of the first two fingers and the thumb of either hand, as I am doing now, and take a deep breath. As I exhale, I will be relaxed and confident.*
- The next time you are talking with your boss. use the Three Fingers Technique, take a deep breath, and relax.
- The final step: Act as if you are relaxed. Make believe if you have to. Pretend. Play like. Make it happen.

Here's how to apply the Three Fingers Technique:

Bring together the tips of the first two fingers and the thumb of either hand, in a circular form.

Not the flat part of the fingers, the tips, the ends of your fingers.

We do this because a lot of energy is radiated out of the tips of the fingers. They are like valves, radiating energy. When you recirculate this energy, you are keeping it from escaping, and you are building it up within you. Then you can program with more energy.

You don't have to use any pressure. Just touch your fingertips together.

In the conditioning cycle, we will program that by bringing together the tips of the first two fingers and the thumb of either hand. Your mind adjusts to a deeper level of awareness for stronger programming.

Stronger programming of information results in easier recall, producing a better memory.

Then we will program two ways that you can use to program yourself to make a stronger impression of information on your brain neurons so that you will remember it better.

We will also program the Test Taking Technique, which uses three steps, including ESP, to help you get the answer you need when you need it.

You can retrieve information that you have impressed on your own brain neurons. You can also detect information that has been impressed on another person's brain neurons.

A Two-Step Programming Technique

To read a lesson, enter level 1 with the use of the 3 to 1 Method. Tell yourself mentally that you are going to count from 1 to 3 and at the count of 3 you will open your eyes and read the lesson. Mention the lesson title and subject.

Add: *Noises will not distract me, but will help me to concentrate. I will have superior concentration and understanding.* Count from 1 to 3, open your eyes, and read the lesson.

When you have read the lesson, once again enter level 1 with the 3 to 1 Method. Tell yourself mentally, *I will recall the lesson I have just read (mention title and subject) anytime in the future with the use of the Three Fingers Technique.*

A One-Step Programming Technique

To hear a lecture, enter level 1 with the 3 to 1 Method, and tell yourself mentally that you are going to hear a lecture and mention the title, subject, and lecturer's name.

Tell yourself that you are going to use the Three Fingers Technique. Keep your eyes open during the lecture.

Tell yourself that noises will not distract you, but will help you to concentrate; that you will have superior concentration and understanding; and that you will recall the lecture (mention title, subject, and lecturer's name) anytime in the future with the use of the Three Fingers Technique.

Observations from José Silva

Here is a short transcription of a recording of José Silva and his thoughts on this:

Notice that for reading, you prepare yourself before—program yourself—because you are going to open your eyes and focus.

Focusing your eyes requires beta brain frequency. So you have to prepare yourself.

You have to sandwich in what you are going to get. Before (pre-) and then post-, program yourself. "I am going to read the lesson," and mention subject name, and title, whatever. Like you are classifying it, so you will know where it's at, what to look for.

Then you come out of your level, and read the lesson.

After you have read the lesson, enter your level again and strengthen the programming. "The lesson I have read, if I need to recall it any time in the future, this lesson (title, and subject matter), all I need to do is to do this (Three Fingers Technique) and it will be fresh in my mind."

So you have two different ways of programming:

- To read a lesson, program before, and again after you have read the lesson.
- To listen to a lecture, use one hand or the other during the lecture.

Retrieving Information When You Need It

For test taking with the Three Fingers Technique, follow the Three Cycle Method:

1. Read your test questions the way you always do, but do not stay too long on any of them. If you have a ready answer, put it down; if not, skip that question and move to the next one.

2. Use the Three Fingers Technique, and do as in the first cycle, but stay a little longer on the unanswered question. When an answer comes, put it down; if not, skip that question and move to the next one.

3. Use the Three Fingers Technique, read the unanswered question, and if still no answer comes, close your eyes, turn them slightly upward, visualize or imagine your professor on your Mental Screen, and ask for the answer. Then clear your mind, and start thinking again to figure out the answer. The answer that comes is your professor's. Write it down. Do not turn in a blank paper.

    In order to clear your mind, think of an entirely different subject for a moment. For instance, after you imagine asking your professor for the answer, think about the chores you have to do later. Then come back to the question, but this time expect an answer. The answer that comes is your professor's. Write it down. Do not turn in a blank paper.

More Ways to Use the Three Fingers Technique

This technique, like all the others, has applications far beyond the examples given here.

When you are going to a meeting, use your Three Fingers Technique to help you remember what you need to remember and respond in the most appropriate and beneficial manner.

If you get into a disagreement with a family member, use your Three Fingers Technique to help you remain calm, understand what the real problem is, and take the most appropriate action, so that everyone will be satisfied.

It is best if you preprogram for the specific situation. For instance, if you get into arguments from time to time, go to your level and analyze the problem. You will get more ideas at your level than you will at beta. Perhaps you will understand the real reason that is causing the arguments. That alone may be enough to solve the problem.

But if you are concerned that you may get involved in another argument, then preprogram yourself with the Three Fingers Technique so you will respond the way that you desire.

Many Silva lecturers, especially when first starting out, program themselves that they will say the right thing at the right time when presenting the course. We program to serve the needs of the people in the class. We also program to answer questions in a way that helps the people who ask them.

You get the idea about how you can use this technique.

In Test Taking step 3, you learn how to use local ESP to detect information that has been impressed on your teacher's brain neurons so that you can get a higher grade on the test. With practice, you can learn how to detect distant information in a similar manner when you are talking with someone, even with your eyes open.

Remember that whenever you focus your eyes, or attempt to focus your eyes, your brain adjusts to beta. If you want to be in alpha with your eyes open, you must defocus them—in sort of a daydreaming state. This takes some practice.

Remember to practice the fundamentals first. Get the techniques working the way you are being taught. Practice the memory pegs to improve your visualization and imagination. Practice entering your level three times a day so that you become so familiar with being at alpha that it will be easy for you to be at the alpha level any time, even when you are active and have your eyes open.

It is one thing to program yourself to have a better memory. That just involves retrieving information impressed on your own brain. But to detect information that is stored on someone else's brain cells involves your mind. It is your mind, in the subjective dimension, that detects the information. You may be able to develop the ability to do that naturally, on your own. We'll talk about how you can learn to do that in the final chapter.

Creating a Life-Saving Technique

Mr. Silva modified the Three Fingers Technique for his son Tony when he was drafted and sent to serve in the Vietnam War.

He explained that it would be difficult to keep the tips of your three fingers together when you are fighting or firing a rifle. So Mr. Silva programmed a different way.

He had Tony press the little finger into the palm of his hand. This is what happens naturally when you make a fist. It is also an easy position when you are firing a rifle: Your forefinger is on the trigger, and you can hold the tip of your little finger against the palm of your hand.

He preprogrammed that whenever Tony held the little finger of either hand against the palm of that hand, he would be more intuitive and aware of any dangerous situation.

How did the technique work? It worked great! Tony told me a story about coming to a fork in the road and selecting one path over another. Later he learned that there were Vietcong soldiers waiting to ambush them on the path they avoided.

Mr. Silva programmed about thirty young men from Laredo along with his own son. The area that they were sent to had such a bad reputation that when new soldiers arrived, the paperwork was prepared for their Purple Hearts, the award they get when they are wounded, with only the date left blank. But all of the young men from Laredo, using their "Little Finger in the Palm of the Hand Technique" came home safely.

Whenever any of these young men would see Mr. Silva on the street, they would wave to him with the little finger folded down into the palm of their hand.

The Three Fingers Technique has become our Silva salute. Graduates all over the world may speak different languages, but they all understand the Three Fingers salute. Whenever you see somebody wave to you with their three fingers together, wave back the same way. You know they are a Silva graduate.

When you are ready, go to appendix C for the information to impress and program the Three Fingers Technique.

SEVEN

Unleash Your Genius Mind: Visualization and Imagination to Solve Problems and Create Solutions

The Mirror of the Mind is one of the most used techniques in José Silva's Choose Success Master Course. It is used for correcting problems and achieving goals.

The Mirror of the Mind uses visualization and imagination, two faculties of genius.

It is very simple to use. Let me tell you how it works, and then we'll talk about some of the ways that you can use it to help you choose success. To use the Mirror of the Mind, here's what you do:

While at your level, create and project on your Mental Screen a full-length mirror. This mirror will be known as the Mirror of the Mind.

This Mirror of the Mind can be mentally increased in size to encompass within its frame a thing or things, a person or persons, a small scene or a large scene.

The color of the frame of the Mirror of the Mind can be mentally changed from blue to white. The blue frame will denote the problem or the existing situation, which can be converted into a project. The white frame will denote the solution or goal.

To solve a problem or to reach a goal with the Mirror of the Mind, enter level 1 with the 3 to 1 Method, then project the image of the Mirror of the Mind with blue frame on your Mental Screen.

Create an image of the problem thing, person, or scene and project it on your blue-framed Mirror of the Mind in order to make a good study of the problem.

After making a good study of the problem, erase the problem image, move the mirror to your left, change the mirror's frame to white, and create and project a solution image onto the white-framed mirror.

From then on, any time you happen to think of the project, visualize the solution image you have created, framed in white. And this is so.

Using the Mirror of the Mind

What can you use the Mirror of the Mind for?

You can use it for anything, when you know what the problem is and you know the solution.

This is not a technique for gathering information. This is a programming technique for correcting a problem. You can use Dream Control step 3 to obtain information.

You can enter your alpha level and analyze information and come up with creative ideas for solving your problem.

Once you have a solution in mind, you use the Mirror of the Mind to program to achieve that solution or to reach that goal.

For instance:

- If you have a health problem, visualize it in the blue-framed mirror; then in the white-framed mirror, imagine yourself in perfect health. From then on, whenever you happen to think of your health condition, recall the solution image you have created, framed in white.

- If you have something that you must learn, such as a test you must take or a new skill you need to develop, then in the blue-framed mirror, visualize yourself studying to learn it. In the white-framed mirror, imagine the test with a perfect score, or imagine yourself doing the new task correctly.

- If you are having family problems—with your spouse or children—mentally picture the problem in the blue-framed mirror; and in the white-framed mirror, imagine everything going smoothly. From then on, whenever you think of the situation (the "project"), recall—visualize—the solution image that you have created, framed in white, and expect the situation to go the way that you desire.

- If you want a promotion, in the blue-framed mirror, visualize yourself in your present position, and in the white-framed mirror, create a mental picture of yourself in your new job.
- If you have having trouble paying your bills, that's what you visualize in the blue-framed mirror. In the white-framed mirror, imagine all of the bills paid. Notice that I did not say to imagine yourself getting money. Getting the money is the problem. In the white-framed mirror, go straight to the solution: in this case, the bills being paid.

Well, you get the idea of what kind of projects you can work on.

Why the Future Is to the Left

You might be wondering why we instruct you to move the mirror to the left.

During his age regression and progression research with children, Mr. Silva found that they were detecting the images of the past towards their right and images of the future to their left. So he incorporated that into the programming.

Program to Solve Problems and Achieve Goals

You notice that in José Silva's Choose Success Master Course, we do not just program for something that we want. We program to solve a problem. That's done throughout the course. For example:

- "I have a headache. I feel a headache. I want to be wide awake, feeling fine and in perfect health."

- "I am drowsy and sleepy. I want to be wide awake."

  With the Mirror of the Mind, we have two ways to indicate that we are moving from a problem—or the existing situation—towards a solution that will follow:

- We move the mirror from its position in front of you towards your left, which is consistent with what Mr. Silva found in his research.

- We change the color of the frame of the mirror from blue to white.

  Many people are "blue" when they have a problem—sometimes "black and blue." When they are worried and depressed, we say that they have the "blues." They "sing the blues."

  So we'll take the blues away and shine a lot of bright white light on our solution. We want to make the solution so bright that it stays in our consciousness all the time, to remind us to keep working towards the solution until we manifest it in the objective dimension, the physical dimension.

Let Your Results Guide You

Once you program, you should see some results within the next three days or so.

If you are making progress towards your goal, towards the solution image you have created in the white-framed mirror, then continue on.

If not, then analyze the situation at your level and make any adjustments that seem appropriate.

You certainly do not want to give up on your programming too soon, but if you are not getting results, then you want to alter your approach in some manner and see if that produces results. Always let your results guide you in your programming.

Be sure to get your body involved. Your mind is not physical, so it cannot do the work in the physical world. The Mirror of the Mind can guide you and keep you focused and heading in the correct direction, but it cannot do the work for you in the physical world.

How to Use the Mirror of the Mind

Mr. Silva envisioned using the Mirror of the Mind to correct all kinds of problems. Let's look at some examples:

- Perhaps you are in a dead-end job. Or you don't have a job; you are unemployed. That's a problem.
- Maybe you love to play golf, but when you play in the club tournament, you seem to make more bad shots than normal. That's a problem.
- Maybe you lack the confidence to stand up for your rights or ideas, and you let people take advantage of you. That's a problem.

Some people are goal-oriented and like to approach things in terms of reaching goals. If that's the case with you, you can use the Mirror of the Mind Technique to help you get anything you'd like to have, do whatever you want to do, and be what you want to be.

We are both saying the same thing, in two different ways. So whether you are like Mr. Silva and are motivated internally to want to correct problems, or, like many other people, you are motivated externally by goals that you can strive for, you can use the Mirror of the Mind to help you get there.

- You can program to get a promotion or a new job.
- You can program to learn new skills.
- You can program yourself to be more confident, more assertive, friendlier, happier—whatever you desire.

Suppose you want a promotion, or a new job. You can program yourself with the Mirror of the Mind to learn whatever you must learn and develop the qualifications necessary to help you get the job. In the blue-framed mirror, visualize yourself in your current job. In the white-framed mirror, imagine yourself in your new job.

Your clairvoyant abilities are also incorporated into the programming, to whatever extent you have developed them.

Once you have programmed for this, you should see signs in the physical world that you are moving in the direction of your goal. When you see that, then continue programming in the same manner, going in the same direction.

Suppose you want to win a trophy in a golf tournament. You can program for that with the Mirror of the Mind. In the blue-framed mirror, picture yourself playing in the tournament. In the white-framed mirror, imagine yourself getting the trophy.

Remember to get your body involved: swing some golf clubs and correct your mistakes so you will continue getting better and better.

In your next golf tournament, you should do better. Perhaps you will win. Even if you don't win, but you do better than you did in the past, then you know that you are moving in the correct direction. Continue to program in the same manner, and you will reach your goal.

If you do worse, or if there is no change, then enter your level and analyze the situation. Perhaps you need to alter your goal. Or you might need to alter your programming in some manner: program more, program less, work on your desire, whatever. The idea is to try something different, and notice how it works. When you are getting good results and moving in the direction of your goal, then you continue doing what you are doing. Let your results guide you.

If you want to be more assertive, first visualize yourself in the blue-framed mirror, backing down and not standing up for your rights or your beliefs. Then in the white-framed mirror, imagine yourself being assertive, standing up for your rights or your beliefs, and imagine people responding positively to you.

Again, let your results guide you. If you are not satisfied with the progress you are making, try something different. When you are satisfied with your progress, continue on.

Always remember that after you program a project for the first time, then whenever you happen to think of the project, visualize the solution image you have created framed in white. Do this any time you happen to think of the project—while programming, while working, while driving.

You do not want to add energy to the problem, so you do not go back to the blue-framed mirror. When you think of your situation, immediately visualize the solution image you have created, framed in white.

Get Your Feelings Involved

Also remember to get your feelings involved. The primary language is visual, and you can add a lot of power to your programming by getting your feelings involved. This is a good way to increase your desire, and the more desire you have, the greater your chances of success.

For instance, imagine how you will feel in your new job. Imagine your satisfaction at the opportunity to be of more service and help more people. Will you feel proud? Get your feelings involved.

How will you feel when the trophy is presented to you for winning the golf tournament? Imagine all of the people watching as you are recognized for your accomplishment. How will that feel?

How will you feel when you stand up for yourself and people accept your ideas and when they do right by you? Will it be a feeling of confidence? Of satisfaction?

Whenever you have a success, then at your earliest opportunity, enter your level and review the success. Especially recall the feeling of success: the feeling you got when you were successful.

There is a special feeling that comes with success that you cannot get any other way. Review it. Establish points of reference so that when you are programming for new projects, you will be able to recall this special feeling of success. This will help your mind adjust to the same level again, so that you will be just as successful in your new project, and even more successful.

It is important to remember what we discussed at the beginning of this course: we are not here just for ourselves; we are here to help correct problems. The more people who benefit, the stronger our desire will be.

In addition, Mr. Silva believed that if we want to get help from higher intelligence, then we have a much better chance if we are doing things that will help more than just ourselves.

Mr. Silva had his own unique way of expressing it. Here is what he said to Silva lecturers and lecturer candidates during an instructor training session in Laredo. He had been explaining that you can get whatever you need as long as it is in the "possibility area." Here is what he said:

How to Qualify for Help from Higher Intelligence

You are asking a good question.

He's asking for a Rolls-Royce. This is in the possibility area.

But you see, we were not sent, we're not going to get help from the other side when we want something like this only for me.

But if I say, I want this vehicle, that we can use—*we*, not just *me*—because there is a need for something like this, and it's within the possibility area, and I don't have the means, I may then get the other side to help me.

Now the other side will only help me when I am asking for something that is needed to improve conditions on planet earth.

Like we said, they are not going to help me if I want another million dollars when I already have a million dollars, when I want a Rolls-Royce when I have a Rolls-Royce already. That I want a girlfriend when I already have a wife. Some people ask for something like this.

They are not going to help you. You are on your own. If you make a mistake, you are going to suffer for it, you are on your own. You don't get help from the other side.

You only get help from the other side when your intentions are that whatever you are doing is to help improve conditions on the planet for more than yourself, not just yourself.

If you only consider *me, me*, you have to do it on your own. If it is for us, then you get help, if whatever you do is going to help more than you.

The more you are going to help, the more help you get for it.

We always say, don't ever ask for more than what you need, but do ask for no less than what you need.

So what your needs will be, depends on how big your plans are. That's what your needs will be.

How to Deal with Fear, Guilt, and Doubt

Now let's talk about what else you can do with the Mirror of the Mind.

You can use it to overcome irrational fear, guilt, and doubt: Irrational fear, guilt about mistakes you may have made, and doubt about your abilities and your value as a human being.

There are three steps:

1. Remove obstacles by neutralizing old traumas.
2. Program at level. Create a blueprint for success.
3. Action in the physical world: do that which you fear.

At your level, you can program to neutralize, rewrite, and change your past history.

Then you can program to succeed in your current activities.

The Theta Brain Wave Level Helps

The theta brain wave level, from 4 to 7 cycles per second, is where we functioned when we were children, from four to seven years old. It is also associated with our survival mechanism.

When we were children, a lot of information was impressed on the theta part of the brain, and some of that information could be causing problems for us today.

For instance, our parents might have tried to motivate us by telling us, "Study hard and make good grades if you want to be successful." Most of us made average grades. Does this mean we will only be average in life?

We cannot function deductively at theta, only inductively. We can take in information at theta, but we cannot activate our mind to make decisions.

A hypnotic operator can take you to theta with conscious awareness and can program you while you are in theta. But you cannot program yourself while you are producing theta brain waves.

However, if you have learned to enter theta on your own with conscious awareness, you can alter information and correct theta-level problems from neighboring alpha.

How to Neutralize Negative Past Programming

When you desire to program to neutralize a limiting belief system, proceed in the following manner:

Enter your level, and use the Mirror of the Mind.

Visualize your problem in the blue framed-mirror directly in front of you.

What is the problem?

Perhaps the problem is that you are not closing enough sales. Perhaps you come right to the close and then back off and lose the sale. Or maybe you come close to your quota, but stop making appointments for the rest of the month. Something stops you from achieving the results you feel that you should be making.

You do not need to figure out why you have the problem. Just figure out what the problem is. Make a good study of it; notice the details. Perhaps you lose your concentration as you near your quota. Maybe you have more errands to run than usual. Maybe you say the wrong thing when asking for appointments. Study the situation, and notice the details.

After you have made a good study of the problem, erase the problem, move the mirror towards your left, change the frame to white, and create and project the solution image onto the white-framed mirror.

What is the solution? The solution might be getting the appointments and making the sales. The solution might be closing successfully and getting the money.

When you do this, you are giving instructions to your mind to find the cause of the problem and correct it. Perhaps the problem was something that a long-forgotten teacher or coach told you. Perhaps it was a prospect who made you feel inadequate.

Whatever cause is, your mind will deal with it. You may become aware of it, or perhaps you will never learn what the cause of the problem was.

When You Do It Yourself, the Change Is Permanent

The key is to you enter your level on your own, not guided by somebody else. Once at your level, you program yourself.

When someone else programs you, results are usually only temporary. When you program yourself, results are usually permanent.

You can also imagine many people benefiting from the solution. The more people who benefit, the better.

Exaggerate your solution, that will give it more energy.

Anytime in the future when you think of this project, visualize (recall) the image that you created of the desired end result in the white-framed mirror.

How Often to Program for a Project?

Remember what we said earlier about the answer to most questions being in the formulas themselves.

The formula tells us, "Whenever you think of the project, visualize the solution image framed in white."

One you create the solution image at your level, the problem is solved . . . in the subjective (mental) dimension. If you go to level and do it again, that implies that you don't believe that the problem is solved.

Since "mind guides brain and brain guides body," you want to keep the solution in mind, not the problem, so any time—any time at all—when you happen to think of the project, visualize (recall) the solution image, framed in white.

If you get additional information and need to incorporate that into your programming, then enter your level and create a new project. If you do not make any progress, enter your level, analyze the situation, and then create a new project.

My Increasing Mental Faculties Are For Serving Humanity Better

It has been said that we need to be able to love and respect our-selves before we can love and respect others. That is the essence of all religions: Do unto others only what you want them to do to you. Love thy God with all thy heart and soul and mind, and love thy neighbor as thyself.

How can you love your God, whom you can't see, if you cannot love and respect your neighbor—the Creator's highest creation—whom you can see?

When you are working on your own problems, keep in mind that one of the reasons you want to improve is so that you can be more helpful to others, so that you can be a better spouse or parent or employer or employee or whatever else you are.

You can program yourself at deep levels to overcome fear, guilt, and doubt so that you can fulfill your mission in life.

If you don't, you might pass on your problems to others, like your own children, and lower their chances of success.

That's what happened to a Silva graduate that I'll call Lee.

Healing Childhood Traumas

Lee would achieve a certain amount of success but would even-tually end up stalled at some point. He might make a mistake or simply be unable to learn something that he was required to learn. Or he would offend the wrong person.

After Lee learned the Silva techniques, he began to use the Mirror of the Mind to go back to his childhood and change things.

When he was young, he was spanked and beaten almost every day until he was a teenager. He went back and in the blue-framed mirror recalled what those beatings were like.

Lee recalled the details: He remembered how the pain would take his breath away. He would experience total panic and hysterics, fearing that he would not be able to breathe, which would cause his death, of course. This, on top of unbearable pain, was a situation far worse than most adults would ever experience. Imagine being severely beaten and fearing permanent injury and perhaps even death, and you will get the idea of his feelings when he was being beaten—almost every day.

Lee used the Mirror of the Mind and in the white-framed mirror imagined a different kind of punishment, something that would still deliver the message that he had done wrong. Lee also imagined that his parents spent time with him, helping him to figure out ways to handle situations that were getting him into trouble. It is very difficult for a young person, with only limited life experience, to know how to say no to his or her friends—people he spends much of the day with—when that means that they might exclude you from the group and even torment you and maybe physically assault you.

So Lee imagined his parents helping him develop strategies to cope with difficult situations and choices that he encountered.

He worked on his fears he still had, such as the apprehension he often felt when working with other people.

He used the Mirror of the Mind to rewrite situations that he felt guilty about. Often while at deep levels, he gained insight and understanding about what had happened and why. This helped to ease the guilt that he felt.

One night, while at a very deep level, thinking about a good friend whose mother had died when he was very young, Lee suddenly realized that there was a similarity between his friend's experience and his own mother's experience. Lee's mother was orphaned at a young age, when her mother died of pneumonia. Her father traveled most of the time, so she grew up in a boarding house, with people who were not even relatives.

Lee realized at that deep level, that this must have left his mother feeling abandoned by both parents. As a result, she must have felt unwanted, unworthy, unloved, and unlovable.

Feeling this way, she must have doubted that anyone worthwhile would *ever* love her, not even her husband. And if she had such a low opinion of herself, how could she ever think any more of her own children? They came from her, so she must have felt that they too were unworthy. No wonder she criticized Lee so much and was so hard on him, so disdainful of his efforts. Deep within herself, she felt unworthy, unloved, and unlovable, so she projected those same characteristics onto her children.

This was a tremendous revelation to Lee. He said, "That helped me to realize that I was not the one who was at fault. I was not a bad person. I was just a little child, who had a right to be loved, and nurtured, and guided. *She* was the one who felt unloved, unworthy. It was *her* problem, not mine!"

Lee said that the next day, he felt wonderful, as though a great burden had been lifted off his back. He said that he has felt more relaxed and has felt much better about himself, and that people are definitely responding better to him. Now he usually does things right. Instead of offending people, he makes them feel good, so they want to be around him.

For the first time in his life, Lee feels that he is accepted by other people and that his opinions are worth listening to—and people *are* actually listening to him. This was very rare before, he said.

This was the second major breakthrough that Lee had experienced. In analyzing the experiences, there seemed to be three factors in common:

- He was at very deep levels,
- Thinking about someone else and their situation,
- And trying to figure out some way to help them.

Deep levels . . . thinking of somebody else . . . and desiring to help them. Then suddenly he realized that his efforts could also be applied to him and his own situation.

This is in line with what José Silva always teaches.

1. Learn to enter the alpha level. Establish a deep level, and learn how to stay there and function there.

2. Do your thinking at alpha. Analyze problems there. There is more information available to you at alpha than at beta, and when you have enough information, it is easy to correct the problem.

3. Mr. Silva says that if you have a problem to work on, find five other people with the same problem, and program for them. If you want to imagine yourself confident, find five other people who also want to be more confident, and program for them. In the white-framed mirror, picture them functioning in a confident manner. That image will also help you to be more confident. It is easier for most people to believe that somebody else can achieve the goal than that they themselves can. So program confidently

for those five people as well as for yourself, and you will multiply your results many times over.

When you do this at very deep levels, then the wounded child within will get the healing that it needs.

Evidently, that's what happened in Lee's case.

Programmed Dreams Help

Dr. Clancy D. McKenzie, a psychiatrist who has been a consultant to the Silva organization since 1970, has had great success in helping people deal with traumatic past events and negative programming.

He simply teaches them how to use the Silva Dream Control Technique step 3 to program a dream that will help them solve their problem.

He has been using this to help combat veterans deal with Post-Traumatic Stress Disorder (PTSD) since the 1970s.

He said that the same approach has helped more than 5,000 patients deal with depression and schizophrenia that is often caused by early childhood traumas, such as a separation from mother trauma.

There is more information on this in our *Silva UltraMind Systems Persuasive Thoughts* book, published by G&D Media and available from booksellers worldwide.

Your Future Is in Your Hands

You now have in your hands the power to change your life.

You now have the tools that you need to choose success.

Review this course from time to time. It is packed with information that will help you to succeed.

And most importantly: *practice, practice, practice.*

Remember what our purpose is: to help correct problems on the planet. This includes your own problems of course. You must prepare the vehicle. You are a vehicle, and in order to be the best problem solving agent that you can be, you need to have your own life under control. But always keep your motive in mind: *helping to correct as many problems as you can.*

Program to correct a problem that affects both you and someone else. Program for both of you. For all of you.

Enter your level every day, once, twice, three times a day, and then get your body involved, get out into the world and take action to achieve your solutions. You must have objective feedback to know that your programming is working.

If you program to be more confident, go out and *be* more confident.

Let your results guide you. Program in a way that you would expect to produce some kind of progress, some result, within two or three days.

If things get better, then you know that you are on the right track. That's the way that our helpers on the other side let us know that we are going in the correct direction.

If you program for something and you encounter a problem, solve the problem and continue on. When you encounter another problem, solve it and continue on. But notice if it took longer to solve the second problem than the first. If it did, take note of that. When you encounter a third problem, if it takes twice as long to solve it as it did to solve the second problem, and it took twice as long to solve the second one as the first, the other side is telling you that you are going in the wrong direction.

On the other hand, if the second problem takes only half as long to solve as the first, and the third takes only half as long as the second, then continue on, full speed ahead. The other side is telling you that you are on the right track. Keep on going.

For a free video demonstrating the Mirror of the Mind technique go to the web page SilvaESP.com/csv/ and use the voucher CSV22 for instant access.

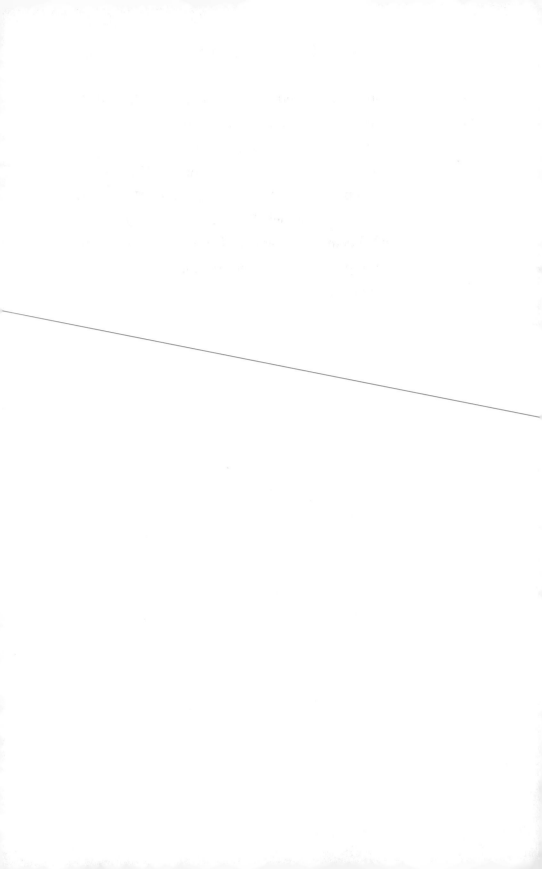

EIGHT

Hand Levitation and Glove Anesthesia

In the next mind training exercise, we will cover two new techniques. You will learn:

- Another way to enter your level, a way that is good to use when you are dealing with past negative programming and traumatic events.
- A first aid technique, called Glove Anesthesia that you can use to relieve pain and often to control bleeding and hemorrhaging. It can also help you to speed the healing process.

You have already learned several ways to enter your level.

First, you learned how to use the Silva Centering Exercise, which you can practice to learn to enter very deep levels of mind.

Then you learned how to enter an alpha state of mind with the Three Fingers Trigger Mechanism. This is the quickest way of all.

Now let's talk about Hand Levitation, another way to enter your level.

Hand Levitation guarantees that you will enter deep levels of mind and low brain frequencies all the way to the theta brain wave level.

Entering level with Hand Levitation is very simple, although it may take you a few minutes to do it in the beginning. The technique was originally developed by a hypnotist named Milton Erickson so that his patients could take themselves to level. This would relieve him of some of the time involved, since he would not have to work with them for as long simply to get to a deep level.

Mr. Silva modified the technique to suit our purposes. Here's how it works:

You start this exercise sitting upright in a chair, with both hands resting in your lap, palms down.

You start at your stronger hand: your dominant hand. If you are right-handed, this means your right hand.

Your goal is to use your imagination to cause your hand to rise from your lap all by itself. You imagine it rising up to touch your face—without any conscious effort on your part.

The subconscious (which you have actually converted into an inner conscious level) causes it to rise at the direction of your imagination.

When your hand comes up all by itself, this confirms that you are at your correct level. It confirms that you have lowered your brain frequency all the way to 5 cycles theta.

There are two ways you can do it.

If you make a recording of the directions, you can use it to go through a practice session before you do it for real. Or you can read the instructions below and then do it without the recording to guide you.

The first time you practice this technique, you will consciously help your hand rise up in order to show your brain what you want it to do.

After you have programmed it at level in this manner, you can practice on your own—without the recording—until your hand comes up all by itself.

Concentrating on a single thing is one of the most common ways to get into a meditative state. When you concentrate totally on your hand, and exclude everything else, your brain, which will be totally bored, will slow down to the theta frequencies, 5 cycles per second. Your concentration actually causes you to enter your level.

When your hand comes up by itself, this confirms that you have indeed entered the theta level.

Now remember, this first time you may have to raise your hand consciously. This is what I want you to do.

Here are the instructions for you to follow. If you are recording this, the script we use in class is in appendix D.

Hand Levitation Instructions

Begin by finding a comfortable sitting position with both hands resting on your lap. Then stare at your stronger hand and cause it to feel sensitive, very sensitive. Then slowly cause one finger to move, then cause your fingers to separate from one another and at the same time cause your hand to rise from your lap."

Now I expect you to do that. If it doesn't happen on its own this first time, then you do it consciously.

Feel your arm becoming lighter and lighter as the back of your hand draws closer and closer to your face. Your hand may feel as though a balloon is lifting it.

Allow your hand and arm to become still lighter and lighter as you continue to help them rise higher and higher.

When the back of your hand touches your face, close your eyes, take a deep breath, and while exhaling, return your hand to its resting position on your lap. You will then be at a deeper, healthier level of mind, deeper than before.

Then you can use the routine deepening techniques, the various statements, and so forth.

Then you can program the new information: program that you have learned *how* to enter level 1 with the Hand Levitation method, and that you may use Hand Levitation to enter deeper, healthier programming levels."

After we have programmed it into your biocomputer brain in that manner, then later, when you have time (allow yourself fifteen or twenty minutes), you can go somewhere by yourself, where you will not be disturbed, and do it for real.

That is, stare at your hand until it comes up all by itself. In the beginning, you might want to help it get started. That's OK. Help it get started, and then it will continue to rise on its own.

For a free video demonstrating the Hand Levitation and Glove Anesthesia techniques go to the web page SilvaESP.com/csv/ and use the voucher CSV22 for instant access.

The Value of Entering the Theta Level

If all of our programming is done at alpha, then why do we want to learn to enter the theta level with conscious awareness?

Because the problem that you desire to correct must be within reach. Your mind must be able to get the necessary information about the problem and correct it. If you have never entered the theta level with conscious awareness, it is closed off to you. It is not within reach.

Entering the theta level with conscious awareness opens it up for you and brings it within reach.

What kind of problems might be rooted at theta?

Limiting belief systems could be rooted there.

You see, children function at much slower brain frequencies than adults. The predominant overall brain frequency of a child of five years of age will be 5 cycles per second. Impressions are made at very low frequencies.

If a five-year-old child is told that they are clumsy or stupid, they simply accept it. At that age, the child only reasons inductively, not deductively. The child does not analyze information but simply records it on their brain cells.

When these levels are within reach, you can enter your level and use the Mirror of the Mind to program yourself to accomplish your goals. If the problems—the limiting belief systems—are rooted in theta, your mind can correct them.

There is more information on this in our *Silva UltraMind Systems Persuasive Thoughts* book published by G&D Media and available at booksellers throughout the world.

Pain Control and Accelerated Healing

There is another reason for opening up the theta levels and bringing them within our reach from the alpha level: biological intelligence is rooted at theta. While psychological health problems are rooted at 10 cycles alpha, where human intelligence resides, other health problems that are rooted at theta, where biological intelligence resides.

That's why hypnotists are able to use the 5 cycles theta level to prepare patients to have teeth pulled, even to have surgery, without the use of chemical anesthetics.

With practice, you can learn to influence biological intelligence.

Your body knows how to heal itself. When you cut your finger, your body knows how to cause the cells to grow back together again.

I'm not saying that you never need a doctor. If it is a big cut, the doctor can sew it up so that there will not be a scar. Antiseptics can be used to keep it from getting infected. But the actual healing process is carried out by your body. Doctors are often important, even vital, to the healing process because they can remove any interference to healing, allowing nature to take its course.

Doctors create an environment that makes it easier for the body to heal. They can keep you alive long enough for the healing to take place.

Now while your doctor works from the outside in, you can work from the inside out to help your doctor heal your body.

You can do many things to speed the healing process besides the frequent advice from doctors to "take an aspirin, get plenty of rest, and call me in the morning."

How does your body know how to heal itself?

Instructions were programmed into your biocomputer brain by whoever originally created and programmed it. Those instructions are part of your biological intelligence. They are automatic. But it is possible, at the correct level, to change those instructions, to take them off automatic and assume manual control.

During his research, José Silva found that a subject's healing mechanism can be fooled during hypnosis.

He says that you can tell the subject that they are going to be touched with a red-hot piece of metal. Then you can touch them with the eraser of an ordinary pencil, and their body will respond as if it were a red-hot iron. The skin will turn red, and a real blister sometimes forms.

Somehow the hypnotist and the subject have influenced the body's healing mechanism to go into action, even though there is no need for it.

We can also learn to alter our perception of pain. Pain is a message that there is a problem. After you receive the message, there is no need to keep the messenger.

Glove Anesthesia

Glove Anesthesia is a formula-type technique that you can practice to develop control of physiological pain and in many cases control of bleeding and hemorrhaging.

Glove Anesthesia is the development of a feeling that is different from the normal. It is usually developed on the less strong of the two hands. If you are right-handed, that will be your left hand.

It could be a cool or cold feeling, or a feeling such as a tingling sensation, a vibration, as though your hand is asleep, as though you have a leather glove on your hand, as though your hand is made of wood, as though you have no hand. Any feeling other than the normal will be considered to be Glove Anesthesia.

Here's how you program Glove Anesthesia on your own.

Sit in a chair. When you begin, make sure that there is some space on each side of your chair, because you are going to imagine placing your hands, one at a time, into imaginary buckets of water that are on each side of your chair.

Then enter your level, do some deepening, and when you are ready continue as follows.

Imagine placing your stronger hand into an imaginary container of hot water standing by your side; the water is hot, and you can stand the temperature. Go through the motions and drop your hand to the side of your chair as if you were actually placing it into a bucket of hot water.

Then bring back a memory of a time when you had your hand in hot water before—any time you can recall vividly After a few moments you can lift your hand out of the hot water, and let it rest on your lap.

Next place your other hand into a container of ice water with cracked ice that is standing by your side. Lower your hand into the imaginary container of ice water with cracked ice standing by your side. Recall a time when you had your hand in ice water. Feel the ice water and cracked ice between your fingers. Feel your hand icy cold.

While your hand is getting colder and colder every second, you can review the first ten memory pegs to improve visualization by using the Mental Screen.

Next, while keeping your eyes closed, lift your hand out of the ice water, and place it over and behind your head, keeping your hand from touching your head. Let your hand dry and get colder in this position. Continue to keep your eyes closed.

When you are ready, bring your hand down, place it on your lap, and test it for coldness and insensibility with your other hand.

After you have done that, remove all abnormal feeling from your hand by rubbing it three times with your other hand, from the wrist toward the fingers like you do when you remove a glove, bringing all feeling back to normal.

Your hand will now feel as it did before the exercise.

As soon as you learn to develop Glove Anesthesia, and after testing it and becoming satisfied with the results, start practicing the transferring of this anesthesia to other parts of the body. First practice transferring this anesthesia from one hand to the other by placing the anesthetized hand over the other hand for a few seconds, then test the other hand for anesthesia. Place it directly on the back of your other hand to transfer the anesthesia.

When this has become effective, practice transferring the anesthesia from either hand to any other part of the body. This is done by placing either hand over that part of the body and holding it in that position for a few seconds. With practice, you can learn to program yourself so that by concentrating on any discomfort and mentally saying the word "Gone," the discomfort will be gone.

You may reinforce the effects of this formula by practice.

To correct health problems, controls are applied under a doctor's supervision.

Using Glove Anesthesia

Glove Anesthesia is an excellent first aid kit, which will be with you all the time. If you are injured, just place your anesthetized hand over the injured area, directly on it if you can, and expect the pain to go away. It will decrease and stop, bleeding will often stop, and you will heal more quickly.

Remember, any feeling other than the normal one will be considered to be Glove Anesthesia. When you let your hand hang down for a long period, then hold it above your head, it is bound to feel different. This is all it takes. Even if it does not feel anesthetized at the time, the programming will still work later on. When you are injured, and the need is real, that *need* will provide the something extra that will make the technique work.

There was a retired man in Florida who had never needed the Glove Anesthesia technique and had never used it until one night he happened to be in a convenience store when it was robbed. The robber tied up the people who were in the store, and when he found that there were only a few dollars in the cash register, he got angry and started stabbing people.

He stabbed the retired man in the chest, and doctors said that the tip of the blade actually punctured his heart. The man had completed the course, but had never used Glove Anesthesia. He couldn't place his hand over the wound because his hands were tied behind his back, so he repeated the words "Pain gone, pain gone."

When he got to the hospital, doctors were amazed that he had lost so little blood. They said the injury should have caused him to bleed much more than he did. They said it was a miracle that he survived.

There are two outstanding techniques for you to practice. When you have become accustomed to entering the theta level, it will be an easy matter to get to alpha any time you desire. You do want alpha functioning to be available to you at any time, don't you?

One Christmas Eve, I decided it was finally time to buy a Christmas present for my sister. I didn't know what to get her, but I was out of time. So I used my level. I found a bench on the sidewalk facing the busy shopping center parking lot, loaded with last-minute Christmas shoppers, cars and people all around, horns blowing, people rushing, lots of noise. I sat on the bench and went to my level.

There is more information available to us at alpha than there is at beta. We can access more of the information stored in our memory banks, which can give us valuable clues about what to do. And we can detect information clairvoyantly.

Despite all the noise and activity, I got the information that I needed. I knew what to get for my sister. I got it and gave it to her the next day. She never knew that I hadn't spent many hours and weeks thinking and planning for the perfect gift. I did it in a matter of minutes—at the alpha level.

It was easy for me to get to alpha, because for several months, I had used Hand Levitation to enter my level almost every day. I still used the 3 to 1 Method also. I was going to level two or three times a day, so I had plenty of opportunity to practice both ways. It paid off for me, and it will for you too.

These are additional tools that you can use. As always, the choice is yours. You can choose to watch television or you can choose to practice. If you are serious about choosing success, you know what to do. Remember, you only have to make one choice at a time. You can do whatever you want to do tomorrow. So what are you going to do today? Are you going to make that one choice and choose success? I hope so.

NINE

Mental Rehearsal for Better Performance

Here's another self-programming technique that you can use to help you correct problems and achieve goals.

The Silva Mental Rehearsal Technique is for practicing skills mentally so that you can perform them better physically.

You can use this in addition to the Mirror of the Mind or instead of it. As always, let your results guide you.

When you use the Mirror of the Mind, you step outside of the scene, so to speak, and observe the scene. By doing this, you can watch yourself in a detached manner. It is like watching a movie of yourself.

With the Mental Rehearsal Technique, you are totally involved. You are right there doing it—not observing yourself doing it, but *doing* it.

Let's say that you want to program yourself to be more assertive. You have several techniques that you can use:

You can do it verbally. Enter your level, state the problem, state the goal, make a plan, work the plan, and get your results, just as you would with the Headache Control or Awake Control techniques.

Or you can incorporate visualization and imagination by using the Mirror of the Mind. Create a picture of the problem in the blue-framed mirror. It can be a moving picture. After making a good study of the problem by observing how you act and react, you erase the problem and create a solution image in the white-framed mirror.

With the Mental Rehearsal Technique, you can go back to the actual situation. You can relive it, you can go through the experience again. Then you can imagine acting differently. For example, you can imagine being more assertive. This can be very beneficial, because you are doing it mentally, with your imagination, instead of physically, with another person involved.

The Mirror of the Mind is like watching a movie of somebody doing it. The Mental Rehearsal Technique is as if you are doing it yourself. In one case, you are the audience; in the other, you are the participant.

With the Mental Rehearsal Technique, you may find it easier to get your feelings involved.

Recall the feeling of being intimidated, for instance, if this happens to you.

Then, as you rehearse mentally (or use the Mirror of the Mind), imagine the feeling you get when you stand up for yourself.

Whenever you use the Mental Rehearsal technique, it is important for you to know the correct way to perform. If you are not sure of what you should be doing, do not use this technique, but use the Mirror of the Mind, where you just create a mental picture of the final end result.

A Case Study

For instance, you may need to make a speech, to give a talk to a group of people. This is one of the biggest fears that people have.

With the Mirror of the Mind, you could watch yourself making an excellent speech. You can sit back and relax, so to speak, and enjoy your performance. You simply program that kind of image (at your level) in the white-framed mirror, and do all that you can to prepare for the speech so that you will be fully prepared when you deliver it. There are several techniques that can help you to do this: memory pegs, the Three Fingers Technique, and so on.

On the other hand, if you know what it's like to deliver a good speech, then you can mentally practice it at your level. Imagine yourself facing a group of people and talking to them; imagine their response to you as they watch you and make eye contact with you. If you know what to expect from your audience, Mental Rehearsal can be a powerful tool.

This is what I had to do to become a Silva lecturer: At my level, I used to imagine speaking before a group of five people. That's the biggest group I could imagine at the time. I imagined that I was presenting the Silva Mind Control Method. I already knew what to say and how to say it; I'd watched other lecturers do it, and I was doing it myself, although I was quite nervous. At first, I did this using the Mirror of the Mind, because it was less threatening to imagine that I was watching a movie of someone (me) performing.

After I became comfortable using my imagination to lecture to five people while at my level, then I imagined a larger group: a group of ten. Gradually I began to imagine presenting the Silva techniques to larger and larger groups. As I became more comfortable with the idea, I imagined that I was facing the audience rather than watching a movie of myself facing an audience. I became the speaker.

During this time, I was getting up and talking to people: to the graduates in our Silva cottage group and to anybody else who would listen.

As part of my training to become a Silva lecturer, my instructor was even allowing me to precondition some of the techniques in the class. I was nervous, but he was there to back me up.

Finally one day, while I was mentally lecturing to a large group—about fifty people—at my level, I realized that my attitude was wrong. I was always concerned about whether *I* had said everything *I* was supposed to say, when in fact I should have been asking myself if *the people in front of me* knew what they needed to know in order to be successful with the techniques.

I changed my attitude immediately. From that time on, I have not focused on myself, which creates great stress, but have focused on the needs of my audience. I'm not up there to make myself look good; I'm there to help the people who have come to the class.

Mental Rehearsal for Fitness and Sports

We also teach this Mental Rehearsal technique in the Silva Star Athlete program. It is a wonderful way to improve physical skills such as athletic performance.

If you are going to use this technique to improve your athletic performance, first, before you enter your level to program and rehearse mentally, make strong points of reference about every aspect of the task as you perform it *physically*. Get your coach to help you.

You can actually go to the place where you practice and go through a practice session. Pay special attention to how you feel as you go through each moment. Make an impression of how it feels when you are one quarter through the movement. Make an impression of how it feels when you are halfway through the movement or exercise. Do the same thing three-quarters of the way through, and again at the completion of the movement.

If you want to improve your golf swing, first you will physically make an impression of exactly how it feels when you address the ball.

How does it feel when you start your backswing? Halfway through your backswing? At the top of your backswing?

Make these impressions throughout your swing as you are actually swinging the club.

When you do this, have your coach there to make sure that you are doing it correctly.

Repeat this for every movement: your chip shots, putts, and so on.

Make impressions of where you are now and where you want to go. Then at your level, you can imagine yourself correcting mistakes and improving your performance.

Keep making these impressions as you go, impressions at each step. Later, just recall the feeling, and you will be there, feeling as though you have practiced, as though you had actually done the movements, even though you did them only at your level.

Once you have made the impressions physically, you can practice at any time you desire, even lying in bed. By doing this, you get the benefits of practice but without fatiguing your body.

While at your level, bring back and visualize the feeling that you had when you performed the movements physically, and your body will respond the same way.

It is important to get your feelings involved. This is a very powerful way to program.

In order to make strong impressions of the special feeling of success, as soon as possible after you have a success, enter your level, and while at your level, review your performance, and recall how you felt when you were successful. This will help you to be even more successful in the future.

Combine Techniques

You can mix and match techniques and find what works best for you. You can always start with the Mirror of the Mind to program your desired end result and then use Mental Rehearsal to help you achieve it.

For instance, if you are in sales, you can use the Mirror of the Mind to imagine yourself being named salesperson of the year. Imagine a picture in the company newsletter of you getting the award. Imagine watching a video of yourself getting the award.

Then you can use Mental Rehearsal to improve your selling skills. There are many other techniques that can help you as well:

- You can use the memory pegs and the Three Fingers Technique to help you remember the features and benefits of your product.
- You can preprogram the Three Fingers Technique to help you stay calm, or be enthusiastic—whatever you need—and to project a confident image when you are working. Or to remind you that your main goal is to help your customer and to be fairly compensated for doing so.

- You can use the self-management techniques to help you get a good night's sleep, wake up on time, and manage your energy.
- You can use the appropriate techniques to get information that will help you to do your job better, such as Dream Control and simply thinking about your project at the alpha level.

Coming up on the next two chapters are additional techniques that will help you:

- Habit Control, to get rid of bad habits that could be holding you back, and create good habits that can help you reach your goals.
- The Mental Mentor, for encouragement and inspiration whenever and wherever you need it.

TEN

Stop Bad Habits and Start Good New Ones

Habits can be your best friend—or your worst enemy.

Let's talk about habits: what they are, how they work, what gives them their power—and how you can change them. You can eliminate bad habits that may be holding you back and start new habits that can help make choosing success automatic!

Habits are patterns of behavior that are repeated over and over again until they become automatic. It is easier to do them than not to do them.

In other words, once you get used to doing something, any effort to change and do something else is very threatening. If you are accustomed to failing, the prospect of succeeding can be very threatening—so threatening that you find a way to fail.

The good news is that once you understand this, you can use the extra energy that's generated to your advantage and turn fear into victory. Let's see how this works.

Habits are powerful because they build on a natural human trait: the apprehension that is triggered anytime we encounter something new or do something different. Or, to say it more simply, fear of the unknown.

This apprehension creates energy that you can use to help you achieve your goals. Or it can create fear that can cause you to crawl in a hole and hide. The choice is yours. You can use this energy any way you desire.

Back before recorded history, in a time when our ancestors had to survive in the jungle without tools or weapons, living by their wits, they developed very strong survival mechanisms.

Imagine them walking through the jungle and hearing a rustling in the bushes nearby. That noise could mean one of two things:

Perhaps it is a small animal, like a rabbit, that they can catch and eat.

Maybe it is a large animal, like a tiger, that wants to catch them and eat them.

It is all a matter of survival. Catch the rabbit and eat it, and you will survive longer. Outrun the tiger, and you will survive.

Either way, our ancestors needed a big burst of energy. The people whose bodies could generate the most energy quickly in an emergency were the people who survived.

Their descendants, including you and me, inherited the characteristics of their ancestors, including the ability to create a lot of energy when something happens that they are not expecting.

That's one reason that habits are so powerful: they are so familiar.

Many habits are very helpful to us. You probably don't even notice which leg you put into your pants first or how you tie your shoelaces. These are things we do automatically, by habit. It makes life easier for us.

Some other habits are not so good for us.

All too often, people embrace habits that relate in some way to the survival mechanism and use these habits to ease and reduce feelings of apprehension.

What are the greatest needs that we have in order to survive?

- We need food every few weeks.
- We need water every few days.
- We need air every few minutes.

When we feel threatened, we have a natural tendency to seek something to reassure us that we can continue to survive, so we ingest food, liquids, air into our body.

Some people eat when they are under stress. High-calorie foods seem to work best—the ones high in sugars and fats, the ones that add the most weight, the ones that have little nutritional value.

Some people drink when they are under stress. When they drink intoxicating liquids, they get the added benefit of a chemically induced feeling of euphoria. Sometimes they even drink themselves into a stupor, where they have no recollection of whatever is causing them stress.

Some people seem to have such a great need for reassurance that they ingest smoke into their lungs, and when they breathe out, they can actually *see* their breath. No wonder smokers get upset when you suggest that they stop smoking. Not only are they addicted to the nicotine and the physical movements involved—handling the cigarettes and so on—they also feel that we are attacking their breath—their very right to breathe! Well, we're not, of course.

Now let's see what you can you get rid of bad habits and create helpful new habits.

José Silva has developed strategies to help you make the changes a little at a time. Small changes are usually easier to make than big ones.

Another strategy is to make the change mentally first, and then the physical change will be automatic.

Let's look at some specific examples, and then we will go to José Silva for the specific formula-type techniques that he developed.

Always Analyze Problems at Level

The first step is always to enter your level to analyze the problem at the alpha level. That is the strongest part of the brain, so use it.

If the problem is cigarette smoking, analyze and determine when you smoke the first cigarette of the day. Is it when you first wake up? With your cup of coffee? While you are on your way to work? Program yourself, at your level, to smoke the first cigarette one hour later.

You are not depriving yourself of the cigarette; you are just changing the habit. In effect, you are developing a new habit by smoking the first cigarette one hour later. And it is easier to break a new habit than an old one. An old habit is so familiar that it can be very difficult to part with. It is like a longtime love affair, and breaking up can be difficult. So do it little by little.

You can change habits in other ways too. For instance, smoke a different brand of cigarette. This makes it a new habit, which will be easier to break.

You can also program yourself to smoke only one cigarette per hour on the hour. When this has become effective, then program yourself to smoke only on the even hours. After this has taken effect, it will, again, be a simple matter to stop smoking completely.

Here is a technique so powerful that it has helped cigarette smokers, drinkers, heroin addicts, and others, to end their habits in thirty days. I've personally met and talked with four people who told me that they were on heroin when they took the Silva Course.

They were so addicted that they would go into the restroom and inject heroin during the breaks in the course!

They got off heroin in thirty days with this technique. Two of those people were so grateful that they became Silva lecturers. One of them won the President's Cup, the top award that José Silva presents to lecturers.

How do they kick this terrible habit?

They do it at level first.

Here's how they did it.

First, mark a date on a calendar thirty days from the present. Then enter your level and tell yourself mentally that on that date, you will stop smoking and will never smoke again in your life. Enter your level every day and reinforce this programming. When the thirty days are up, you will not want to smoke anymore.

You can apply this technique to any kind of habit.

Other tips that can help you to stop smoking:

- Change brands frequently.
- Do not inhale the cigarette smoke.
- Program that 3 deep breaths will stop the immediate desire to smoke.
- Stop smoking for the sake of your loved ones.

Create New Beneficial Habits

You can create new habits in the same manner. Do them gradually.

If you want to get into the habit of going to level every morning when you first wake up, in the beginning you might have to remind yourself to do it. You might have to rearrange your schedule a bit. Make it easy on yourself by going to level for just five minutes.

When this becomes effective, then begin staying at level for ten minutes. When this is easy and natural, increase to the recommended fifteen minutes.

Whenever you do something every day, you *condition yourself* to do it every day. You make it a habit. So pay attention to the habits you create, and make sure that all of your new habits are good habits.

What habits do successful people have?

Start studying successful people, the kind of people that you admire and that you would like to be like. What do they do? What are their regular habits?

Perhaps they get up earlier in the morning so that they can get some work done before other people start calling on them and interrupting them.

Maybe they have the habit of calling business associates or clients or a regular basis. Maybe they set aside fifteen minutes every day for such "service calls."

Maybe they exercise on a regular basis, because they know that in order to do the amount of work they must do to achieve the level of success they desire, they need a strong, healthy, and fit body.

Whatever habits they have, you can develop too.

Make the changes and start these news habits on the inside first. Program them at your level. Do them at level every day. This is easy; there is no stress involved. There is no stress when you imagine calling people on the phone. After you get used to doing it at your level, you will find that it will be easy to do it objectively— physically—as well.

Program yourself at your level for thirty days that you will practice a regular exercise program. By that time, you will find that you are just as comfortable with the new habit that you have done at your level as you are with the old physical habit. It will be a simple choice. You can choose the habit that you want.

Willpower Never Wins

One word of caution: you cannot change habits with willpower.

Whenever willpower and imagination are in conflict, imagination always wins.

Let's take a simple example. Suppose you are determined to eat more nutritious food so that you will remain healthy and will have the energy that you need to do the work required to be as successful as you desire to be. As always, it is your choice.

So you go into a diner with a group of friends. They all order big meals, but you only order the chef's salad, with the dressing on the side.

All goes well until time for dessert.

Whenever willpower and imagination are in conflict, the imagination always wins.

The good news is:

You can use your imagination to increase your willpower.

At your level, program for what you desire. Get your imagination and your willpower working together.

Dwell on what you desire: the good health, the feeling of energy.

Remember how we started this course by talking about how important it is that you have a purpose, that you have reasons for doing what you are doing?

At your level, review the reasons that you have for wanting to change your eating habits, or to exercise more regularly, or to stop smoking or drinking, or whatever you want to change. Then come up with more reasons.

Do it for your family's sake if you have no other reason. Do you want your children to imitate you and smoke or drink or lose their temper and get into trouble? Do you want to take the chance of having a heart attack and having your family go on without you? This might be enough motivation for you to take whatever steps are necessary to change your habits.

Small Changes Make It Easier to Succeed

Remember what we mentioned about changing habits little by little.

Sometimes you might find it better to change only the part of the habit that causes actual harm. That may be as far as you can go at that time.

José Silva suggests that if you are accustomed to handling cigarettes with your hands, holding them between your lips—and all of the other little activities that are associated with cigarette smoking—go ahead and do those things, but just don't inhale the cigarette smoke.

Drinkers can do the same thing by drinking nonalcoholic beer or wine. At first it may taste a little different, but before long you will grow accustomed to it.

How do I know? Well, I used to drink a little beer. OK, more than a little. At the age of thirty, I was drinking at least half a case of beer every night. Now I have no desire to drink any alcoholic beverage. In fact, I cannot even imagine why I would want to impair my senses in the slightest!

But I drank so much beer for so long that after I stopped drinking it, I felt strange in many situations. Watching a football game, for instance, I longed to have my hand around a cold beer can. I wanted to enjoy the feel of the cold, carbonated liquid flowing down my throat and enjoy the taste. It is an acquired taste: it is pretty awful when you first start, but if you are persistent, you can learn to love it, just like a person who gets sick the first time they try smoking a cigarette but who gets so addicted that they can't stop.

Now I can have all of that thanks to the nonalcoholic beers that are available.

José Silva suggests using a glass of tomato juice spiked with a liberal amount of hot pepper sauce whenever you have the urge to drink. Mr. Silva says that this is a good way to work on drinking and drug habits. Just be sure to consult with your doctor and make sure it is safe for you to use the hot sauce.

I found a substitute when I stopped drinking coffee, a beverage that I never really liked anyway and has no nutritional value.

I used to drink about forty cups a day! I missed having it there with me when I was working, so I began to drink herbal teas.

Or better yet, a drink that I have offered to many people (if I just give it to them matter-of-factly, they think it is some kind of chicory coffee): blackstrap molasses in very hot water.

My molasses drink tastes similar to coffee, and it is hot. I drink it in my coffee cup. There are so many similarities that I satisfy all of the old familiar aspects of drinking coffee—without drinking coffee. You get the idea.

Weight and Habit Control Procedure

This next formula covers techniques for weight control, followed by techniques to help you stop smoking. You can use these techniques for any other habits.

Here's how it goes:

When you desire to reduce weight, enter level 1 by the use of the 3 to 1 Method, and analyze your weight problem. At level 1, mentally mark a big red *no* over every item of food considered to be causing the problem.

Program yourself that hunger between meals will vanish by eating a piece of carrot, celery, or apple, or some such helpful foods, or by taking three deep breaths.

Have an "instead of." This is a very valuable thing. If you remove the habit and do not replace it with anything else, the habit will come back.

You can replace bad habits with the desire to be healthy, for instance. You can also replace them with other habits until you get to the point where you no longer have a need for the habit at all.

Taking three deep breaths is another way of ingesting something into your body. So is drinking water.

You can program yourself to leave something on your plate, realizing that you do not need all the food you have taken. Program yourself not to eat dessert.

Visualize yourself in the blue-framed Mirror of the Mind the way you are now. Then in the white-framed mirror, stamp what you want to weigh on one corner and the size of suit or dress you want to wear on the other corner, and imagine yourself at your ideal weight and size.

Thereafter, when you think of your weight, always visualize the image you have created of yourself the way you want to be in the white-framed Mirror of the Mind.

Whenever you are eating, visualize the image you have created of yourself the way you want to look in the white-framed Mirror of the Mind, and visualize your desired weight stamped on one corner and your desired size of clothing stamped on the other corner.

If you desire to gain weight, eat those foods that you sense at level 1 will help you gain. Eat slowly, savoring every bite. Learn to improve your taste and smell by concentrating on your food as you eat.

Use the Mirror of the Mind and visualize yourself the way you want to be. Do this every time you think of your weight.

Let Your Results Guide You

There are many techniques and suggestions here because each person is different and responds in a different way. Find something that works for you, and stick with it.

If one technique doesn't give you the results you want, try another one.

The choice is yours. If you really want to choose success (remember to enter your level and review your reasons for desiring to succeed), you will use the tools that we are providing in this course.

They work. If these techniques work for heroin addicts, for smokers, for alcoholics, they will work for you too.

In a research project, fifteen recovering alcoholics in a halfway house all took the course. Six months later, twelve of them had not had another drink! One had a few drinks and stopped on his own. Another drank for a couple of days and then stopped. Only one needed intervention to help him stop. That's considered a tremendous success rate for hard-core alcoholics.

Do what they did: use your level—the powerful alpha level—to provide you with a choice: to drink or not to drink.

And remember: It works for drug addiction too.

ELEVEN

Call on Expert Help
Whenever You Need It

It is very valuable to have support systems in your life. You need people who understand you, love you, and support you and your efforts.

In the Silva program, we emphasize many kinds of support systems:

- Graduate meetings
- Cottage group meetings
- Silva graduate support groups
- The buddy system
- Programming partners

You can even have a subjective support system, which is the purpose of the technique in this chapter.

Back in 1966 and '67, when José Silva first began teaching Silva Mind Control in the Texas Panhandle, he found that graduates were supporting one another. They often lived so far apart that they weren't getting together for meetings, he said, but whenever somebody in the group needed help, they spread the word, and everybody went to work to program for them and help them.

This is the essence of a support group: people who sincerely want to help one another.

We have private forums for Silva graduates on the SilvaESP. com website. If you'd like to participate, use the contact information on the website to let us know, and we'll get you set up.

We started a support group here in Laredo, more or less by accident. It turned out to be the most valuable thing I'd been involved with since I first took the course fifteen years earlier.

I'd come to the office once a week and open up, but that's all I did. I left it up to graduates to decide what to do in our meetings. What we did was talk with each other: we'd gossip, we'd share our successes with each other, we'd talk about our problems and projects and goals and hopes and dreams. We got to know each other intimately.

Then we'd arrange the chairs in a circle, and somebody would read the Long Relaxation Exercise to take us all to level together. Once we had entered a deep level, we'd go around the circle, giving each person an opportunity to ask for help in programming any project or projects that they had.

We got spectacular results. Everybody was benefiting tremendously. I didn't even know what a support group was, but here we had established one. One of the group members explained to me that Alcoholics Anonymous was a support group, so I got a copy of the Alcoholics Anonymous book and read it. It really excited me.

Support Group Case Study

Here's one example of how we helped one another: One member of our group was trying to sell his house. He had programmed every detail, imaging somebody coming to look at the house, making an offer, negotiating, and finally closing the deal.

But nothing was happening.

After we had all been to level together one night, another group member said, "Maybe you are trying too hard. Maybe you need to keep it simple."

The next week, the man with the house for sale reported that he had sold it. "I took your advice," he told the group member who had suggested that he simplify his programming. "I just imagined pulling up the 'For Sale' sign and throwing it away because the house had been sold."

We were spending so much time at level together and programming for each other every day that we got to know each other really well and could offer insights like that all the time. Everybody was benefiting greatly.

I realized just how valuable everybody felt our support group was when group members decided to hold our regular meetings—which we held every Wednesday—even though they would fall on Christmas Day and New Year's Day. Did we think that our support group was valuable to us? You bet!

Your Own Personal Support Group

Eventually I started traveling so much that I could not keep up with the group meetings. My support group became a programming partner. We would each go to level at ten o'clock every evening and program for each other.

We talk with each other a couple of times a week, to get feedback on the programming we are doing for the other person, so that we can make any adjustments that are indicated. This has worked great for us.

And you know what's really interesting? That idea did not come from José Silva or anyone at Silva international headquarters. It did not come from any of our lecturers. It came from a Silva graduate who was a regular member of our support group. She suggested it, and we've been using it ever since.

Meet Your Mental Mentor

Now here is a technique that José Silva designed especially for this Choose Success Master Course.

The idea is to create, at your level, a subjective (mental) duplicate of your favorite teacher, a person that you admire, someone who has helped you, taught you, and guided you in your life or career.

You can imagine this person encouraging you when you need encouragement. You can imagine them reminding you of successes that you have had to give you confidence that you will succeed in your current projects.

Your Mental Mentor can remind you to remember your points of reference for your successes: how you programmed, how you performed, how you felt, and how it felt when you were successful. These things will help you to be just as successful and even more successful every time.

Remembering your successes is an excellent way to improve yourself. José Silva says that we used to be taught to learn from our mistakes and failures.

Now, he says, brain and mind research has shown us that there is a better way.

Now we know that the best way to achieve great success is to use our smaller successes as stepping stones.

Great athletes do this.

A few years back, a young tennis player named Zina Garrison was playing Monica Seles at Wimbledon. Monica was not yet the number one player in the world: that came the following year.

Zina had lost the first set and was behind in the second set. Monica slammed a ball across the net, and Zina lurched for it. She missed it, fell to the ground, and fell hard. When she got up with her knee bleeding, even watching on television, you could tell she was shaken.

That's a tough spot to be in. To make it worse, it was Monica's advantage. If Monica won the next point, she would win the game. To make it even worse, if she won that game, it would also give her the set and the match. It was match point, as they say in tennis. And Zina had only thirty seconds to compose herself to fight off match point.

Somehow she did and managed to win the point. In fact, she kept winning points and went on to win the game. She continued to play well, pulled even with Monica, and then won the set.

That meant that they had to play a third set to see who would continue on in the tournament, and who would be eliminated.

Zina Garrison won the third set and the match. She eliminated a player who was seeded much higher than she was.

As Zina was walking off the court after the victory, sportscaster Bud Collins stopped her for an interview. He asked her how she managed to collect herself and come back to win the point, and eventually the match, after the bad fall that scraped up her knee so badly.

Zina told him that she just remembered times in the past when she was in a similar situation—when she was hurt and was down at match point—but came back to win the match. She had done it before, so she believed that she could do it again. She was her own role model.

Your will surely have your own inspirational stories, people who have inspired you, times that you have inspired yourself.

Imagine how valuable it will be to remember those positive things when the going gets tough.

Your Mental Mentor can remind you of things like that. Just program it at your level. Then, when you find yourself in a tough situation, imagine what your Mental Mentor would say to you:

"Come on, you can do it! You've succeeded in difficult situations before. Remember how you did it. Remember how you felt. Feel that way again."

You can imagine your Mental Mentor reminding you of all of the benefits of succeeding. Your Mental Mentor can remind you of all of the other people who will benefit when you succeed. Your Mental Mentor can also remind you of how to proceed and what to do each step of the way.

Of course it is great to have a physical mentor too, a person you can call on who can give you ideas and help you.

But in many ways, this Mental Mentor technique has advantages over having a physical mentor. For instance, your Mental Mentor can be with you all the time. And your Mental Mentor will always know exactly what to say to you, because you are in control: you are the one who is choosing—at your level, of course—what your Mental Mentor should say.

It is a great technique, one that will help you a lot.

How to Create Your Mental Mentor

To create your Mental Mentor, create and project onto your Mental Screen a mental picture of this person who has helped you, who is one of your favorite teachers.

Recall what this person looks like: their height and weight, their facial features, the color and length of their hair. Recall how this person moves, their gestures, and how they talk.

Then imagine your Mental Mentor moving away from the Mental Screen and becoming dynamic and fully alive.

You can imagine talking with your Mental Mentor at any time, and imagine how your Mentor would guide you, support you, and serve as an example for you.

Your Mental Mentor can encourage you when you are performing tasks. Simply recall this person and imagine what they would say to you, and use this to help you achieve greater results.

Who do you want for your Mental Mentor? If you are not sure, enter your level and think about it. You will come up with more ideas and make a better decision at your level.

How a New Artist Began Painting Far above Her Level

Here is a transcript of José Silva recalling how he helped a group of artists with a similar concept: a Master Artist to help each of them. This was for the group of artists who were in his very first public class, in Amarillo, Texas, back in late 1966.

They asked, "What else can we do?"

I said, "You can do anything."

"For instance," I said, "you, come here, Mary."

Mary came forward.

I said, "Go to your level. I want to talk to when you are at your level."

"OK, I'm there now."

"You are what, a sculptor or a painter?

"I am a painter."

"Oh, you are a painter?"

"Yes."

She wanted to be a painter. She was not there yet, but was studying. I selected the wrong person. I should have selected a painter who was already a painter, not one just in training.

Anyway, I said, "You should use your imagination on this. Who do you like to paint like?"

"Oh, like Van Gogh."

"Well, great. This is very good. A lot of people like Van Gogh's paintings. Have you read Van Gogh's history?"

Oh, she knows it back and forth. Her idol is Van Gogh. She wants to ultimately paint like Van Gogh.

"Well, all right, let's create a Van Gogh right by your side. How about that?"

"What do you mean?"

"I mean, like drawing one, like sculpturing one. Work on his head, his shoulders . . . create one. A spiritual Van Gogh. Let him be beside you."

She went ahead and did this.

"Have you created, painted, or sculpted a Van Gogh yet?"

"Yes, he is right here right now."

"All right. Now whenever you are painting, and you meet a problem in painting, bring your three fingers together, on one hand or the other, and then imagine Van Gogh, ask him what to do. Whatever comes to your mind is his answer. Follow it up, and continue. Whatever comes your mind is his, transmitting his ideas into your mind, as to what to do. So you'll be thinking as though you thought it up yourself. But you thought it up with the information he gave you. And you follow through, and continue."

So she came out of level, went and got her easel, tripod or whatever, her oils, everybody gathered around—the whole class—and she started to paint.

First she used a pencil and drew—she wanted to draw a vase with flowers, on a table with a tablecloth. She started sketching, then using paints. In no time at all she had a beautiful vase, flowers, and everybody was going, "Wow, look at this, what she's doing. And so fast!" Everybody was amazed.

At this time, Professor Dord Fitz came in. "What's all this commotion about?"

They told him what was happening.

"OK," he said, "let's gather around and analyze the painting and see if it appears like Van Gogh's work."

He liked this kind of work.

He said, "Notice these spots here. Van Gogh used to have the habit of leaving some of the canvas exposed, not covered with paint. Even that's here."

I didn't know anything about this.

The mistake I made: I selected a person who had only had two classes in art. I thought she was one of the advanced students. I made a mistake. Now that's what really turned them on:

"She's doing this! Mary's doing this." She was not supposed to do that with only two lessons in art.

Now everybody wanted me to train them with their Da Vincis, their Rembrandts, and on and on. I got myself a lot of work there because of that. I had to work with each one individually to get them what they wanted, Da Vincis, Rembrandts, and whatever.

Five years later I got them to have an area convention to see how they were doing with the work. Were they really using it?

We had about 600 graduates come out. They would get on stage and tell us what they were doing.

They said, "Well, we don't practice, we don't have meetings and practice, but whenever one of the family members gets injured or sick, everybody helps them at levels."

A woman got up there, a schoolteacher, and I said, "What do you think of the Silva Mind Control?"

"Well, Silva Mind Control is a method of mental training that helps an individual become a better problem solving agent on the planet, a healthier, better problem solving agent on the planet."

Everybody applauded.

An elderly gentleman got up there and said, "What Mind Control means to me is that if I go to church to pray for rain, I take my umbrella with me."

Everybody liked that.

Then this young lady got up there and said, "I think I've got the best message for all of you. I have an invoice here." She was one of the painters in the group. "I sold a painting in Dallas for $26,000."

At one time, they said, "We don't want to do this any more."

I said, "What do you mean?"

"We don't want to be imitations of anybody. We want to be originals. Our own selves. We don't want to be imitators of anybody."

I said, "What's wrong with starting off like a Da Vinci, like a Rembrandt, and go from there? We're not telling you to be a duplicate of them. Use them to move on from there."

They got stuck. They didn't know what to do. They didn't know how to improve over the great artists of the past. We want to go beyond that.

So we said, "Why don't you go from where they left off and continue on, not to be just duplicates of these people?"

They finally said, "OK, we understand what you mean."

That's what this man Jesus said when he came by. He said, "He who believes in me and the works that I do, he also shall do." But he didn't stop there. "Greater than this you shall do." He was just getting started in this field. You should do better than I did.

Same thing here. This works for all these painters also. Better than they have ever done, we should do. They understood then. They continued working in these areas.

So Amarillo was the first place where we started, and every so often we meet some of the graduates when we go there. Sometimes they come and repeat the course here in Laredo.

TWELVE

Your Next Step:
Developing Your God-Given ESP

Congratulations! You have just completed the most advanced self-programming course in the world. Now you can do things that most people only dream about:

- You have learned how to enter the powerful alpha brain wave level with conscious awareness, and how to activate your mind while remaining at the alpha level so that you can program yourself for success.

- You learned how powerful positive thinking is. You also learned practical techniques to help you actually practice positive thinking and maintain a positive mental attitude regardless of what's going on around you.

- You've learned how to go to sleep without drugs and wake up without clocks. You've learned the Awake Control Technique that you can use to remain awake and refreshed longer.

- You have learned how to remember dreams and use them to understand yourself better and to get information to help you make decisions and solve problems.
- You've learned how to use your Mental Screen to help you set and achieve goals.
- You have learned techniques that you can use to strengthen your memory.
- You've learned how to use the Three Fingers Technique for self-programming in order to remember better, and to recall information for tests.
- You learned how to use the Mirror of the Mind technique for self-programming.
- You have learned how to enter the theta level, where you can correct problems rooted at theta.
- You have learned how to control pain and to relieve tension headaches and migraine headaches.
- You have learned techniques to neutralize negative past programming and make room for positive new programs in order to help you overcome limiting belief systems and be more successful.
- You have learned how to practice mentally so that you will perform better physically.
- You have learned how to stop bad habits and to start good new habits.
- You have created a Mental Mentor to inspire and help you.

Imagine how all of these techniques will help you in both your personal life and your career.

In order to continue to learn and improve yourself, your next step is to develop your God-given intuition.

Yet by the age of thirty, he had the largest radio and electronics repair business in South Texas, as well as a nice home, a beautiful family, and lots of friends.

As a child, working in the streets of Laredo, young José had made many good business decisions. His fertile imagination gave him many ideas for ways to serve more people and thereby earn more money. Even though he had no formal business training, he made many good business decisions. He seemed to be able to do the right thing at the right time.

Being on his own, he *had* to make his own decisions. He learned how to trust his intuition—the gut feeling, the small voice within—to make correct decisions.

Actually, all children between the ages of seven and fourteen are creative, imaginative, and clairvoyant. But as they grow up, most of them focus on physical development and the physical world and leave the mental world behind.

José Silva maintained his mental abilities and even expanded on them.

Many other people have done the same thing. But those people have seldom been able to transfer their ability to anyone else.

Very few have actually been able to show anyone else— even their own children—how to do what they did.

They are not able to transfer their special abilities to other people.

It was different with José Silva, because he was different.

At the age of thirty, he made a commitment to help his children to be more successful.

He tried talking with them, as all parents do. He used the same techniques as everybody else: Encouragement, rewards, threats, pleas.

When he was introduced to psychology, he tried that.

When he read how Freud had used hypnosis, he tried that.

Soon he found that by some mysterious means, his own clairvoyant abilities were being transferred to his children!

Actually, before his children began to exhibit their clairvoyant abilities, he didn't even realize that he himself was a clairvoyant.

That's typical. Most of the supersuccessful people believe that they function just like everybody else. So they tell everybody else what they do and cannot understand when most people are unable to do things the way they do.

But José Silva saw the difference in his own children and recognized the difference between himself and most other adults: the difference in the way that he used his mind.

While most people guessed wrong the majority of the time when they had to guess, José Silva's guesses were usually right. Anybody who is right more times than wrong is going to be very successful.

Besides working with his own children, Mr. Silva also worked with other people who asked him for help.

He discovered that he was able to transfer his special abilities to other people besides his own children.

In fact, over several years of research, he found that he could transfer his abilities to *anyone* who wanted them.

He had to do it at deep levels of mind—not by hypnosis; that wasn't reliable.

Instead, he developed his own method of teaching people how to reach deep levels of mind so that he could then transfer his own abilities to them.

This was done with hundreds of people.

But soon he found that thousands of others wanted him to do the same for them: to transfer his intuitive and clairvoyant abilities to them.

There wasn't enough of him to go around.

So he tried a bold experiment.

He took one of the people that he had transferred his abilities to, and trained him to do the same thing: to use his mind to guide other peoples' minds and thereby transfer his newfound clairvoyant abilities to them.

And it worked.

Then Mr. Silva shifted his focus and began to concentrate on training trainers, not only transferring his clairvoyant abilities to them but training them to pass these abilities on to other people.

As a result, tens of thousands of people began to benefit.

Today, Mr. Silva's courses have spread out over the entire world. Millions of people, in more than 100 countries, have benefited.

Mind training doesn't depend on language. Certified Silva instructors present the program in twenty-nine different languages.

Perhaps the most exciting part of the ESP training is the final session, when you work health cases.

You start with just four pieces of information: the name, age, sex, and location of the subject. That's all.

Then you scan the subject's body mentally, the way you learned in the ESP training, and let your mind find the problem areas. With just a little practice, you can learn to focus in on specific health problems.

Then you use your mind to correct those problems, just as you learned to do in this course.

A Transformative Experience

Case working is an exciting, inspiring experience. It immediately confirms that you are at your level and that you are able to detect information at a distance with your mind. You also get the satisfied feeling of knowing that you have helped someone unselfishly. The more you practice, the more people you can help. And the more you practice, the more your own skills will develop.

Eventually you will become so accustomed to functioning at this level that you will begin to do it naturally, almost without thinking about it, any time during the day or night, whenever you need to obtain information. All you will need to do is to recall the special feeling of being at your level and accurately detecting information, and you will be there and will function clairvoyantly.

Now you know the secret of the most successful people on the planet.

"A Blessing on the Human Race"

How valuable is it to develop your mind in this manner? Napoleon Hill—the first person to make an extensive study of successful people and what they did that led to their success—said that the average person's mind stops rising and searching after a certain point. He adds: "The individual who discovers a way to stimulate his mind artificially, arouse it and cause it to go beyond this average stopping point frequently, is sure to be rewarded with fame and fortune if his efforts are of a constructive nature."

Then he added, "The educator who discovers a way to stimulate any mind and cause it to rise above this average stopping point without any bad reactionary effects, will confer a blessing on the human race second to none in the history of the world."

The educator who did it was José Silva.

Now the Choice Is Yours

You can visit the SilvaInstructors.com website for a list of Silva instructors who specialize in ESP training. You can start with one of the ESP home study courses available in both Online Learning and Downloads.

You can use the book *Silva UltraMind Systems ESP for Business Success*, which includes the complete ESP training. The book is published by G&D Publishing and is available from booksellers worldwide. The audiobook version is titled *Silva UltraMind's Intuitive Guidance System for Business*.

Learning to use your ESP reliably and regularly will not only change your life for the better, it will also help humanity move into what José Silva called the "second phase of human evolution on the planet."

Humanity can and *must* find ways to correct the problems that we are facing.

With most people thinking only with their left-brain hemisphere, the problems are getting worse. "Reinventing" government will not correct the problems. Neither will "reinventing" the corporation.

It is not the institutions that are at fault. It is the people who are involved in them. When people are able to use more of their brains and minds, when they know that they can get everything they want for themselves without hurting anybody or taking anything away from anyone else, we can have peace on our planet.

It all starts with a simple choice, and proceeds one choice at a time. No big deal. Just choose success— for yourself, for our planet, and for humanity.

Thank you once again for learning José Silva's Choose Success Master Course and permitting us to work for you and with you.

Please feel free to visit us at SilvaESP.com and let us know how you are doing, and how we can be of service to you.

Choose to keep practicing, to establish your level at very deep levels of mind. Choose to persist and to get each technique working for you. Choose to continue your journey by developing your ESP.

Choose to do these things, and you will be choosing success.

Appendix A

The Silva Centering Exercise by José Silva

The Silva Centering Exercise helps you discover an inner dimension, a dimension that you can use to become healthier, luckier, and more successful in achieving your goals.

When you learn to function from this inner dimension, you automatically become more spiritual, more human, healthier, safer from accidents, and a more successful problem solver.

In order for you to use this inner dimension, you need to hear the Silva Centering Exercise a total of ten hours and to follow the simple directions in the mind exercise.

How to Read the Silva Centering Exercise

When reading the Silva Centering Exercise, read in a relaxed, natural voice. Be close enough so that the listener can hear you comfortably. Read loud enough to be heard, and read as though you were reading to a seven-year-old child. Speak each word clearly and distinctly.

Have the listener assume a comfortable position. A sitting position is preferred, but the most important thing is to make sure that the listener is comfortable. If uncomfortable, the listener will not relax as much and will not get as much benefit from the exercise.

Avoid distractions, such as loud outside noises. There should be enough light so you can read comfortably but no extremely bright lights.

If the person shows any signs of nervousness or appears to be uncomfortable, stop reading, tell them to relax and make themselves comfortable. When they are comfortable and ready, then continue.

Take your time when you read; there is no need to rush.

Note: Do not read the headings (in bold print) or the words in parentheses. They are for your information.

Deepening (Physical Relaxation at Level 3)

Find a comfortable position, close your eyes, take a deep breath, and while exhaling, mentally repeat and visualize number 3 three times. (pause)

To help you learn to relax physically at level 3, I am going to direct your attention to different parts of your body.

Concentrate your sense of awareness on your scalp, the skin that covers your head; you will detect a fine vibration, a tingling sensation, a feeling of warmth caused by circulation. (pause) Now release and completely relax all tensions and ligament pressures from this part of your head, and place it in a deep state of relaxation that will grow deeper as we continue. (pause)

Concentrate your sense of awareness on your forehead, the skin that covers your forehead; you will detect a fine vibration, a tingling sensation, a feeling of warmth caused by circulation. (pause) Now release and completely relax all tensions and ligament pressures from this part of your head, and place it in a deep state of relaxation that will grow deeper as we continue. (pause)

Concentrate your sense of awareness on your eyelids and the tissue surrounding your eyes; you will detect a fine vibration, a tingling sensation, a feeling of warmth caused by circulation. (pause) Now release and completely relax all tensions and ligament pressures from this part of your head, and place it in a deep state of relaxation that will grow deeper as we continue. (pause)

Concentrate your sense of awareness on your face, the skin covering your cheeks; you will detect a fine vibration, a tingling sensation, a feeling of warmth caused by circulation. (pause) Now release and completely relax all tensions and ligament pressures from this part of your head and place it in a deep state of relaxation that will grow deeper as we continue. (pause)

Concentrate on the outer portion of your throat, the skin covering your throat area; you will detect a fine vibration, a tingling sensation, a feeling of warmth caused by circulation. (pause) Now release and completely relax all tensions and ligament pressures from this part of your body, and place it in a deep state of relaxation that will grow deeper as we continue. (pause)

Concentrate within the throat area, and relax all tensions and ligament pressures from this part of your body, and place it in a deep state of relaxation, going deeper and deeper every time. (pause)

Concentrate on your shoulders; feel your clothing in contact with your body. (pause) Feel the skin and the vibration of the skin covering this part of your body. (pause) Relax all tensions and ligament pressures, and place your shoulders in a deep state of relaxation, going deeper and deeper every time. (pause)

Concentrate on your chest; feel your clothing in contact with this part of your body. (pause) Feel the skin and the vibration of your skin covering your chest. (pause) Relax all tensions and ligament pressures, and place your chest in a deep state of relaxation, going deeper and deeper every time. (pause)

Concentrate within the chest area; relax all organs; relax all glands; relax all tissues, including the cells themselves, and cause them to function in a rhythmic, healthy manner. (pause)

Concentrate on your abdomen; feel the clothing in contact with this part of your body. (pause) Feel the skin and the vibration of your skin covering your abdomen. (pause) Relax all tensions and ligament pressures, and place your abdomen in a deep state of relaxation, going deeper and deeper every time. (pause)

Concentrate within the abdominal area; relax all organs; relax all glands; relax all tissues, including the cells themselves, and cause them to function in a rhythmic, healthy manner. (pause)

Concentrate on your thighs; feel your clothing in contact with this part of your body. (pause) Feel the skin and the vibration of your skin covering your thighs. (pause) Relax all tensions and ligament pressures, and place your thighs in a deep state of relaxation, going deeper and deeper every time. (pause)

Sense the vibrations at the bones within the thighs; by now these vibrations should be easily detectable. (pause)

Concentrate on your knees; feel the skin and the vibration of your skin covering the knees. (pause) Relax all tensions and ligament pressures, and place your knees in a deep state of relaxation, going deeper and deeper every time. (pause)

Concentrate on your calves; feel the skin and the vibration of the skin covering your calves. (pause) Relax all tensions and ligament pressures, and place these parts of your body in a deep state of relaxation, going deeper and deeper every time. (pause)

To enter a deeper, healthier level of mind, concentrate on your toes . (pause) Enter a deeper, healthier level of mind.

To enter a deeper, healthier level of mind, concentrate on the soles of your feet. (pause) Enter a deeper, healthier level of mind. (pause)

To enter a deeper, healthier level of mind, concentrate on the heels of your feet. (pause) Enter a deeper, healthier level of mind. (pause)

Now cause your feet to feel as though they do not belong to your body. (pause)

Feel your feet as though they do not belong to your body. (pause)

Your feet feel as though they do not belong to your body. (pause)

Your feet, ankles, calves, and knees feel as though they do not belong to your body. (pause)

Your feet, ankles, calves, knees, thighs, waist, shoulders, arms, and hands feel as though they do not belong to your body. (pause)

You are now at a deeper, healthier level of mind, deeper than before.

This is your physical relaxation level 3. Whenever you mentally repeat and visualize the number 3, your body will relax as completely as you are now, and more so every time you practice.

Deepening (Mental Relaxation at Level 2)

To enter the mental relaxation level 2, mentally repeat and visualize the number 2 several times, and you are at level 2, a deeper level than 3. (pause) Level 2 is for mental relaxation, where noises will not distract you. Instead, noises will help you to relax mentally more and more.

To help you learn to relax mentally at level 2, I am going to call your attention to different passive scenes. Visualizing any scene that makes you tranquil and passive will help you relax mentally.

Your being at the beach on a nice summer day may be a tranquil and passive scene for you. (pause)

A day out fishing may be a tranquil and passive scene for you. (pause)

A tranquil and passive scene for you may be a walk through the woods on a beautiful summer day, when the breeze is just right, where there are tall shade trees, beautiful flowers, a very blue sky, an occasional white cloud, birds singing in the distance, even squirrels playing on the tree limbs. Hear birds singing in the distance. (pause)

This is mental relaxation level 2, where noises will not distract you.

To enhance mental relaxation at level 2, practice visualizing tranquil and passive scenes.

To Enter Your Center

To enter level 1, mentally repeat and visualize the number 1 several times. (pause)

You are now at level 1, the basic level, where you can function from your center.

Deepening Exercises

To enter deeper, healthier levels of mind, practice with the countdown deepening exercises.

To deepen, count downward from 25 to 1, or from 50 to 1, or from 100 to 1. When you reach the count of 1, you will have reached a deeper, healthier level of mind, deeper than before.

You will always have full control and complete dominion over your faculties and senses at all levels of the mind, including the outer, conscious level.

When to Practice

The best time to practice the countdown deepening exercises is in the morning when you wake up. Remain in bed at least five minutes practicing the countdown deepening exercises.

The second best time to practice is at night, when you are ready to retire.

The third best time to practice is at noon after lunch.

Five minutes of practice is good, ten minutes is very good, and fifteen minutes is excellent.

To practice once a day is good, two times a day is very good, and three times a day is excellent.

If you have a health problem, practice for fifteen minutes, three times a day.

To Come out of Levels

To come out of any level of the mind, count to yourself mentally from 1 to 5, and tell yourself that at the count of 5, you will open your eyes, be wide awake, feeling fine and in perfect health, feeling better than before.

Then proceed to count slowly from 1 to 2, then to 3, and at the count of 3, mentally remind yourself that at the count of 5 you will open your eyes, be wide awake, feeling fine and in prefect health, feeling better than before.

Proceed to count slowly to 4, then to 5. At the count of 5 and with your eyes open, mentally tell yourself, "I am wide awake, feeling fine, and in perfect health, feeling better than before. And this is so."

Deepening (Routine Cycle)

To help you enter a deeper, healthier level of mind, I am going to count from 10 to 1. On each descending number, you will feel yourself going deeper, and you will enter a deeper, healthier level of mind.

10—9, feel going deeper,

8—7—6, deeper and deeper,

5—4—3, deeper and deeper,

2—1

You are now at a deeper, healthier level of mind, deeper than before.

You may enter a deeper, healthier level of mind by simply relaxing your eyelids. Relax your eyelids. (pause) Feel how relaxed they are. (pause) Allow this feeling of relaxation to flow slowly downward throughout your body all the way down to your toes. (pause)

It is a wonderful feeling to be deeply relaxed, a very healthy state of being.

To help you enter a deeper, healthier level of mind, I am going to count from 1 to 3. At that moment, you will project yourself mentally to your ideal place of relaxation. I will then stop talking to you, and when you next hear my voice, one hour of time will have elapsed at this level of mind. My voice will not startle you; you will take a deep breath, relax, and go deeper.

1—(pause)—2—(pause)—3. Project yourself mentally to your ideal place of relaxation until you hear my voice again. Relax. (Reader: remain silent for about thirty seconds.)

Relax. (pause) Take a deep breath, and as you exhale, relax and go deeper. (pause)

Rapport

You will continue to listen to my voice; you will continue to follow the instructions at this level of the mind and any other level, including the outer conscious level. This is for your benefit; you desire it, and it is so.

Whenever you hear me mention the word "Relax," all unnecessary movements and activities of your body, brain, and mind will cease immediately, and you will become completely passive and relaxed physically and mentally.

I may bring you out of this level or a deeper level than this by counting to you from 1 to 5. At the count of 5, your eyes will open; you will be wide awake, feeling fine and in perfect health.

I may bring you out of this level or a deeper level than this by touching your left shoulder three times. When you feel my hand touch your left shoulder for the third time, your eyes will open; you will be wide awake, feeling fine and in perfect health. And this is so.

Genius Statements

The difference between genius mentality and lay mentality is that geniuses use more of their minds and use them in a special manner.

You are now learning to use more of your mind and to use it in a special manner.

Beneficial Statements

The following are beneficial statements that you may occasionally repeat while at these levels of the mind. Repeat mentally after me. (Reader: read slowly):

My increasing mental faculties are for serving humanity better.

Every day, in every way, I am getting better, better, and better.

Positive thoughts bring me benefits and advantages I desire.

I have full control and complete dominion over my sensing faculties at this level of the mind and any other level, including the outer conscious level. And this is so.

I will always maintain a perfectly healthy body and mind.

Effective Sensory Projection Statements for Success

Effective Sensory Projection statements for success. I am now learning to attune my intelligence by developing my sensing faculties and to project them to any problem area so as to be aware of any actions taking place, if this is necessary and beneficial for humanity.

I am now learning to correct any problems I detect.

Negative thoughts and negative suggestions have no influence over me at any level of the mind.

Post Effects: Preview of Next Session

You have practiced entering deep, healthy levels of mind. In your next session, you will enter a deeper, healthier level of mind, faster and easier than this time.

Post Effects: Standard

Every time you function at these levels of the mind, you will receive beneficial effects physically and mentally.

You may use these levels of the mind to help yourself physically and mentally.

You may use these levels of the mind to help your loved ones, physically and mentally.

You may use these levels of the mind to help any human being who needs help, physically and mentally.

You will never use these levels of the mind to harm any human being; if this be your intention, you will not be able to function within these levels of the mind.

You will always use these levels of the mind in a constructive, creative manner for all that is good, honest, pure, clean, and positive. And this is so.

You will continue to strive to take part in constructive and creative activities to make this a better world to live in, so that when we move on, we shall have left behind a better world for those who follow. You will consider the whole of humanity, depending on their ages, as fathers or mothers, brothers or sisters, sons or daughters. You are a superior human being; you have greater understanding, compassion, and patience with others.

Bring Out

In a moment, I am going to count from 1 to 5. At that moment, you will open your eyes, be wide awake, feeling fine and in perfect health, feeling better than before. You will have no ill effects whatsoever in your head, no headache; no ill effects whatsoever in your hearing, no buzzing in your ears; no ill effects whatsoever in your vision and eyesight; vision, eyesight, and hearing improve every time you function at these levels of mind.

1-2, coming out slowly now.

3, at the count of 5, you will open your eyes, be wide awake, feeling fine and in perfect health, feeling better than before, feeling the way you feel when you have slept the right amount of revitalizing, refreshing, relaxing, healthy sleep.

4-5. Eyes open, wide awake, feeling fine and in perfect health, feeling better than before.

(Reader: Be sure to observe whether or not the person is wide awake. If in doubt, touch the person's left shoulder three times and while doing so, say: "Wide awake, feeling fine and in perfect health. And this is so.")

It is recommended that everyone practice staying at your center for fifteen minutes a day to normalize all abnormal conditions of the body and mind.

Appendix B

Forty-Day Countdown System for Finding the Alpha Level

I will give you an alternate way to find the alpha level. You can use this instead of the Silva Centering Exercise if you prefer. I will begin by giving you a simple way to relax, and you will do better and better at this as you practice.

I will also give you a beneficial statement to help you.

This is how you train your mind. You relax, lower your brain frequency to the alpha level, and practice using imagination and visualization.

Because you cannot read this book and relax simultaneously, it is necessary that you read the instructions first so that you can put the book down, close your eyes, and follow them.

Here they are:

1. Sit comfortably in a chair, and close your eyes. Any position that is comfortable is a good position.

2. Take a deep breath, and as you exhale, relax your body.

3. Count backward slowly from 50 to 1.

4. Daydream about some peaceful place you know.

5. Say to yourself mentally, "Every day, in every way, I am getting better, better, and better."

6. Remind yourself mentally that when you open your eyes at the count of five, you will feel wide awake, better than before.

When you reach the count of 3, repeat this, and when you open your eyes, repeat it ("I am wide awake, feeling better than before").

You already know steps one and two. You do them daily when you get home in the evening. Add a countdown, a peaceful scene, and a beneficial statement to help you become better and better, and you are ready for a final count-out.

Read the instructions once more. Then put the book down and do it.

Learning to Function Consciously at the Alpha Level

As stated previously, you learn to enter the alpha level and function there with just one day of training when you attend the Silva UltraMind ESP Systems live training programs. You can use audio recordings to learn to enter the alpha level within a few days with either a Silva home study program or the free lessons at the SilvaESP.com/csv/ website. You can also record the Silva Centering Exercise in appendix A and listen to it, or have someone read it to you.

If you have already learned to enter the alpha level by one of those methods, you can skip the following instructions for practicing countdown deepening exercises for the next forty days.

If not, then follow these instructions from José Silva:

When you enter sleep, you enter alpha. But you quickly go right through alpha to the deeper levels of theta and delta.

Throughout the night, your brain moves back and forth through alpha, theta, and delta, like the ebb and flow of the tide.

These cycles last about ninety minutes.

In the morning, as you exit sleep, you come out through alpha back into the faster beta frequencies that are associated with the outer conscious levels.

Some authors advise that as you go to sleep at night, you think about your goals. That way, you get a little bit of alpha time for programming. The only trouble is, you have a tendency to fall asleep.

For now, I just want you to practice a simple exercise that will help you learn to enter and stay at the alpha level. Then, in forty days, you will be ready to begin your programming.

In the meantime, I will give you some additional tasks that you can perform at the beta level that will help you prepare yourself so that you will be able to program more effectively at the alpha level when you are ready at the completion of the forty days.

YOUR FIRST ASSIGNMENT

If you are using the Silva Centering Exercise on the SilvaESP.com/csv/ website to enter the alpha level, you can skip the information that follows.

If you do not want to use the recording of the Silva Centering Exercise, or record it yourself from the script in appendix A, and you have not attended a Silva seminar or used one of our home study courses to learn to enter the alpha level, then you will need to follow the instructions here to learn to enter the alpha level on your own.

Here is your alpha exercise:

Practice this exercise in the morning when you first wake up. Since your brain is starting to shift from alpha to beta when you first wake up, you will not have a tendency to fall asleep when you enter alpha.

Here are the steps to take:

1. When you awake tomorrow morning, go to the bathroom if you have to, then go back to bed. Set your alarm clock to ring in fifteen minutes, just in case you do fall asleep again.

2. Close your eyes, and turn them slightly upward toward your eyebrows (about 20 degrees). Research shows that this produces more alpha brain wave activity.

3. Count backward slowly from 100 to 1. Do this silently; that is, do it mentally to yourself. Wait about one second between numbers.

4. When you reach the count of one, hold a mental picture of yourself as a success. An easy way to do this is to recall the most recent time when you were 100 percent successful. Recall the setting, where you were, and what the scene looked like; recall what you did; and recall what you felt like.

5. Repeat mentally, "Every day in every way I am getting better, better, and better."

6. Then say to yourself, "I am going to count from 1 to 5; when I reach the count of 5, I will open my eyes, feeling fine and in perfect health, feeling better than before."

7. Begin to count. When you reach 3, repeat, "When I reach the count of 5, I will open my eyes, feeling fine and in perfect health, feeling better than before."

8. Continue your count to 4 and 5. At the count of 5, open your eyes and tell yourself mentally, "I am wide awake, feeling fine and in perfect health, feeling better than before. And this is so."

These Eight Steps Are Really Only Three

Go over each of these eight steps so that you understand the purpose, and at the same time you become more familiar with the sequence.

1. The mind cannot relax deeply if the body is not relaxed. It is better to go to the bathroom and permit your body to enjoy full comfort. Also, when you first awake, you may not be fully awake. Going to the bathroom ensures your being fully awake. But in case you are still not awake enough to stay awake, set your alarm clock to ring in fifteen minutes, so you do not risk being late on your daily schedule. Sit in a comfortable position.

2. Research has shown that when a person turns the eyes up about 20 degrees, it triggers more alpha rhythm in the brain and also causes more right-brain activity. Later, when we do our mental picturing, it will be with your eyes turned upward at this angle. Meanwhile, it is a simple way to encourage alpha brain wave activity. You might want to think of the way you look up at the screen in a movie theater: a comfortable upward angle.

3. Counting backward is relaxing. Counting forward is activating. 1-2-3 is like "get ready, get set, go!" 3-2-1 is pacifying. You are going nowhere except deeper within yourself.

4. Imagining yourself the way you want to be—while relaxed—creates the picture. Failures who relax and imagine themselves making mistakes and losing frequently create a mental picture that brings about failure. You will do the opposite. Your mental picture is one of success, and it will create what you desire: success.

5. Words repeated mentally—while relaxed—create the concepts they stand for. Pictures and words program the mind to make it so.

6-8. These last three steps are simply counting to 5 to end your session. Counting upward activates you, but it's still good to give yourself "orders" to become activated at the count of 5. Do this before you begin to count; do it again along the way; and again as you open your eyes.

Once you wake up tomorrow morning and prepare yourself for this exercise, it all works down to three steps:

1. Count backward from 100 to 1.

2. Imagine yourself successful.

3. Count yourself out 1 to 5, reminding yourself that you are wide awake, feeling fine, and in perfect health.

Forty Days That Can Change Your Life—for the Better

You know what to do tomorrow morning, but what about after that? Here is your training program:

Count backward from 100 to 1 for 10 mornings.

Count backward from 50 to 1 for 10 mornings.

Count backward from 25 to 1 for 10 mornings.

Count backward from 10 to 1 for 10 mornings.

After these 40 mornings of countdown relaxation practice, count backward only from 5 to 1, and begin to use your alpha level.

People have a tendency to be impatient, to want to move faster. Please resist this temptation, and follow the instructions as written.

You must develop and acquire the ability to function consciously at alpha before the mental techniques will work properly for you. You must master the fundamentals first. We've been researching this field since 1944, longer than anyone else, and the techniques we have developed have helped millions of people worldwide to enjoy greater success and happiness, so please follow these simple instructions.

Appendix C

Conditioning Cycle to Use When Impressing Formulas

Instructor: Read this material first, then move ahead to the formula or formulas you want to impress, and after reading them move ahead to the Preview/Post Effects/Bring Out.

Note: Do not read the headings (in bold print) or the words in parentheses. They are for your information.

Entry

We will start this exercise with the 3 to 1 Method.

Find a comfortable position, close your eyes, take a deep breath, and while exhaling, mentally repeat and visualize the number 3 three times. (pause)

Take another deep breath, and while exhaling, mentally repeat and visualize the number 2 three times. (pause)

Take another deep breath, and while exhaling, mentally repeat and visualize the number 1 three times. (pause)

You are now at level 1, the basic plane level that you are learning to use for a purpose, any purpose you desire.

Deepening (Routine Cycle)

To help you enter a deeper, healthier level of mind, I am going to count from 10 to 1. On each descending number, you will feel yourself going deeper, and you will enter a deeper, healthier level of mind.

10—9, feel going deeper,

8—7—6, deeper and deeper,

5—4—3, deeper and deeper,

2—1

You are now at a deeper, healthier level of mind, deeper than before.

You may enter a deeper, healthier level of mind by simply relaxing your eyelids. Relax your eyelids. (pause) Feel how relaxed they are. (pause) Allow this feeling of relaxation to flow slowly downward throughout your body, all the way down to your toes. (pause)

It is a wonderful feeling to be deeply relaxed, a very healthy state of being.

To help you enter a deeper, healthier level of mind, I am going to count from 1 to 3. At that moment, you will project yourself mentally to your ideal place of relaxation. I will then stop talking to you, and when you next hear my voice, one hour of time will have elapsed at this level of mind. My voice will not startle you; you will take a deep breath, relax, and go deeper.

1—(pause)—2—(pause)—3. Project yourself mentally to your ideal place of relaxation until you hear my voice again. Relax. (Reader: Remain silent for about thirty seconds.)

Relax. (pause) Take a deep breath, and as you exhale, relax and go deeper. (pause)

Rapport

You will continue to listen to my voice; you will continue to follow the instructions at this level of the mind and any other level, including the outer conscious level. This is for your benefit; you desire it, and it is so.

Whenever you mentally or verbally mention the word "Relax," all unnecessary movements and activities of your body, brain, and mind will cease immediately, and you will become completely passive and relaxed physically and mentally.

I may bring you out of this level or a deeper level than this by counting to you from 1 to 5. At the count of 5, your eyes will open; you will be wide awake, feeling fine and in perfect health.

Genius Statements

The difference between genius mentality and lay mentality is that geniuses use more of their minds and use them in a special manner.

You are now learning to use more of your mind and to use it in a special manner.

Beneficial Statements

The following are beneficial statements that you may occasionally repeat while at these levels of the mind. Repeat mentally after me. (Reader: Read slowly.)

My increasing mental faculties are for serving humanity better.

Every day, in every way, I am getting better, better, and better.

Positive thoughts bring me benefits and advantages I desire.

I have full control and complete dominion over my sensing faculties at this level of the mind and any other level, including the outer conscious level. And this is so.

Protective Statements

The following statements are for your protection.

This is MIND CONTROL, your own self-MIND CONTROL. You are always in control. You may accept or reject anything I say, any time, at any level of the mind. You are always in control.

Preventive Statements

The following preventive statements are for your better health. Keep in mind that from now on, I will occasionally be speaking in your place. (Read slowly.)

I will never learn to develop physically or mentally, mental disorders nor psychosomatic or functional ailments or diseases.

I will never learn to develop, physically or mentally, a dependence on drugs or alcohol.

Negative thoughts and negative suggestions have no influence over me at any level of the mind.

I will always maintain a perfectly healthy body and mind.

Mental Projection Statements for Success

Mental Projection statements for success.

I am now learning to attune my intelligence by developing my sensing faculties, and to project them to any problem area, so as to become aware of any abnormalities, if this is necessary and beneficial for humanity.

I am now learning to apply corrective measures and to correct any abnormality I detect.

Negative thoughts and negative suggestions have no influence over me at any level of the mind.

Reader: At this time, move ahead to the formula/s you want to impress. After reading them, move ahead to the Preview, Post Effects, and Bring Out.

Formula-Type Techniques

SLEEP CONTROL

Impression of information for your benefit, programming a formula-type technique.

Sleep Control, a formula-type technique that you can use to enter normal, natural, physiologic sleep, any time, anywhere, without the use of drugs.

Whenever you need to use Sleep Control, enter level 1 with the 3 to 1 Method. Once at level 1, use the Sleep Control formula-type technique:

In a moment I will count from 1 to 3. At that time, you will visualize a chalkboard. You will mentally have chalk in one hand and an eraser in the other.

You will then mentally draw a large circle on the chalkboard. Then you will mentally draw a big X within the circle. You will then proceed to erase the X from within the circle, starting at the center and erasing towards the inner edges of the circle, being careful not to erase the circle in the least.

Once you erase the X from within the circle, to the right and outside of the circle you will write the word "Deeper." Every time you write the word "Deeper," you will enter a deeper, healthier level of mind, in the direction of normal, natural, healthy sleep.

You will then write a big number 100 within the circle; then you will to erase the number 100, being careful not to erase the circle in the least. Once the number 100 is erased, to the right and outside of the circle you will go over the word "Deeper."

Every time you go over the word "Deeper," you will enter a deeper, healthier level of mind, going in the direction of normal, natural, healthy sleep. You will continue using numbers within the circle on a descending scale until you enter normal, natural, healthy, physiologic sleep.

I will now count from 1 to 3. 1-2-3. Visualize a chalkboard now. You mentally have chalk in one hand and an eraser in the other.

Now mentally draw a large circle on the chalkboard. (pause)

Draw a big X within the circle. (pause) Proceed to mentally erase the X from within the circle, starting at the center, being careful not to erase the circle in the least. (pause)

Once you erase the X from within the circle, to the right and outside of the circle, write the word "Deeper." (pause) Every time you write the word "Deeper," you will enter a deeper, healthier level of mind, in the direction of normal, natural, healthy sleep.

Now write a big number 100 within the circle. (pause) Proceed to mentally erase the number 100 from within the circle, starting at the center, being careful not to erase the circle in the least. (pause)

Once you erase the number 100 from within the circle, to the right and outside of the circle go over the word "Deeper." (pause) Every time you go over the word "Deeper," you will enter a deeper, healthier level of mind, in the direction of normal, natural, healthy sleep.

Now write within the circle the number 99. (pause) Erase it in the same manner. (pause) Now go over the word "Deeper." (pause) Every time you go over the word "Deeper" in this manner, you will enter a deeper, healthier level of mind, in the direction of normal, natural, healthy sleep.

Continue with the numbers 98, 97, 96, 95, 94, 93, and so on, on a descending scale until you hear my voice next. I will now stop talking to you. When you hear my voice next, one hour of time will have elapsed at this level of mind. My voice will not startle you; you will take a deep breath, and you will enter a deeper, healthier, level of mind, deeper than you are now.

Continue with the numbers on a descending scale until you hear my voice again. Relax. (Reader: Wait thirty seconds.)

Relax. Every time you use Sleep Control in this manner, you will enter normal, natural, healthy, physiologic sleep, any time, anywhere, without the use of drugs.

Whenever you enter sleep with the use of Sleep Control, if someone calls you are in case of danger or in an emergency, you will open your eyes, be wide awake feeling fine and in perfect health.

Whenever you enter sleep with the use of Sleep Control, you will awaken at your customary time or assigned time, and be wide awake, feeling fine and in perfect health.

TO AWAKE CONTROL AND AWAKE CONTROL

Impression of information for your benefit, programming a formula-type technique.

To Awake Control, a formula-type technique that you can use to practice awakening without an alarm clock. This helps in your development of mind control. To use To Awake Control, practice awakening without an alarm clock.

You can also learn to use Awake Control to remain awake longer when necessary.

Enter level 1 with the 3 to 1 Method just before going to sleep.

At level 1, visualize a clock. Mentally move the hands of the clock to indicate the time that you want to awaken, and tell yourself mentally, "This is the time I want to awaken, and this is the time I am going to awaken."

Stay at level 1, and go to sleep from level 1. You will awaken at your desired time and be wide awake, feeling fine and in perfect health.

To use Awake Control for learning to remain awake longer.

Whenever you feel drowsy and sleepy and don't want to feel drowsy and sleepy, especially when you are driving, pull to the side of the road, stop your motor, and enter level 1 with the 3 to 1 Method.

At level 1, mentally tell yourself, "I am drowsy and sleepy; I don't want to be drowsy and sleepy; I want to be wide awake, feeling fine and in perfect health."

Then tell yourself mentally, "I am going to count from 1 to 5. At the count of 5 I will open my eyes, be wide awake, feeling fine and in perfect health. I will not be drowsy and sleepy; I will be wide awake."

Count mentally, slowly: 1-2-3. At the count of 3, mentally remind yourself that at the count of 5, "I will open my eyes, be wide awake, feeling fine and in perfect health."

Then mentally count slowly to 4, then 5. At the count of 5 and with your eyes open, tell yourself mentally, "I am wide awake, feeling fine and in perfect health, feeling better than before."

DREAM CONTROL

Impression of information for your benefit, programming a formula-type technique.

Dream Control, a formula-type technique that you can use to practice remembering dreams. This helps in your development of mind control.

To practice remembering a dream, you will enter level 1 with the 3 to 1 Method. Once at level 1, you will mentally tell yourself, "I want to remember a dream, and I am going to remember a dream." You will then go to sleep from level 1.

You will awaken during the night or in the morning with a vivid recollection of a dream. Have paper and pencil ready to write it down. When you are satisfied that Dream Control step 1 is responding, then start with Dream Control step 2.

Dream Control step 2: To practice remembering dreams, you will enter level 1 with the 3 to 1 Method. Once at level 1, mentally tell yourself, "I want to remember my dreams, and I am going to remember my dreams." You will then go to sleep from level 1.

You will awaken several times during the night and in the morning with vivid recollections of dreams. Have paper and pencil ready to write them down. When you are satisfied that Dream Control step 2 is responding, then start with Dream Control step 3.

Dream Control step 3: To practice generating a dream that you can remember, understand, and use for problem solving. You will enter level 1 with the 3 to 1 Method. Once at level 1, mentally tell yourself, "I want to have a dream that will contain information to solve the problem I have in mind." State the problem and add, "I will have such a dream, remember it, and understand it." You will then go to sleep from level 1.

You may awaken during the night with a vivid recollection of the desired dream, or you may awaken in the morning with a vivid recollection of such a dream. You will have this dream, remember it, and understand it.

HEADACHE CONTROL

Impression of information for your benefit, programming a formula-type technique.

Headache Control, a formula-type technique that you can use to practice stopping headaches.

Tension-type headaches, one application; migraine-type headaches, three applications, five minutes apart.

Headache Control, a formula-type technique that you can use to practice stopping tension type headaches. If you have a tension-type headache, enter level 1 with the 3 to 1 Method. Once at level 1, mentally tell yourself, "I have a headache; I feel a headache; I don't want to have a headache; I don't want to feel a headache.

"I am going to count from 1 to 5, and at the count of 5, I will open my eyes, be wide awake, feeling fine and in perfect health. I will then have no headache. I will then feel no headache."

You will then count slowly from 1 to 2, then to 3, and at the count of 3 you will remind yourself mentally, "At the count of 5, I will open my eyes, be wide awake, feeling fine and in perfect health; I will then have no discomfort in my head; I will then feel no discomfort in my head."

Notice that we have made a change at level 3, from "ache" to "discomfort." We left the ache behind. You will then proceed to mentally count slowly to 4, then to 5, and at the count of 5, and with your eyes open, you will say to yourself mentally, "I am wide awake, feeling fine and in perfect health. I have no discomfort in my head. I feel no discomfort in my head. And this is so."

Headache Control, a formula-type technique that you can use to practice stopping the migraine type headache. If you have a migraine headache, enter level 1 with the 3 to 1 Method. Once at level 1, go through the same procedure as in the tension-type head-ache application, but use three applications, five minutes apart.

You will note that the first application will have reduced the discomfort by a certain amount. Wait five minutes, then apply the second application. The second application will take care of a greater amount of the discomfort. Wait five more minutes, and apply the third application. With the third application, all of the discomfort will have disappeared.

From then on, when symptoms appear, one application will take care of the migraine problem. As you continue to take care of this problem in this manner, the symptoms will appear less fre-quently, until the body forgets how to cause them, bringing to an end the migraine problem without the use of drugs. And this is so.

To correct health problems, controls are applied under a doctor's supervision.

Mental Screen

We will now impress new information for your benefit, programming the Mental Screen.

To locate your Mental Screen, begin with your eyes closed, turned slightly upward from the horizontal plane of sight, at an angle of approximately 20 degrees.

The area that you perceive with your mind is your Mental Screen.

Without using your eyelids as screens, sense your Mental Screen to be out, away from your body.

To improve the use of your Mental Screen, project images or mental pictures onto the screen, especially images having color. Concentrate on mentally sensing and visualizing true color.

Memory Pegs

We will now impress and program for your benefit several memory pegs to be used for the improvement of visualization, imagination, clairvoyance, and memory. The practice of projecting the mental pictures of the memory pegs on your Mental Screen will help you to develop the faculty of visualization and imagination, leading to superior clairvoyance.

We will now program ten of the standard and most used basic memory pegs.

No. 1 The letter T, the peg word *Tea*. Project a strong picture of a glass of tea on your Mental Screen. (pause)

No. 2 The letter N, the peg word *Noah*. Project a picture of a man with a long white beard on your Mental Screen. (pause)

No. 3 The letter M, the peg word *May*. Project a picture of a calendar on your screen.

No. 4 The letter R, the word *Ray*. Mental picture: sun rays. (pause)

No. 5 The letter L, the word *Law*. Mental picture: a police officer. (pause)

No. 6 The letter J, the word *Jaw*. Mental picture: a person with a large jaw. (pause)

No. 7 The letter K, the word *Key*. Mental picture: a large gold key. (pause)

No. 8 The letter F, the word *Fee*. Mental picture: a price tag of 8 million dollars (pause)

No. 9 The letter B, the word *Bay*. Mental picture: land and water. (pause)

No. 10 The letters T and S, the word *Toes*. Mental picture: ten toes. (pause)

You have now impressed and programmed memory pegs for your benefit. You may use them for the improvement of visualization, imagination, clairvoyance, and memory.

The Three Fingers Technique

We will now impress information for your benefit, programming a formula-type technique, the Three Fingers Technique. At this time, bring together the tips of the first two fingers and thumb of either hand. (pause)

By bringing together the tips of the first two fingers and thumb of either hand, your mind adjusts to a deeper level of awareness for stronger programming.

Stronger programming of information results in easier recall, producing a better memory.

To read a lesson, enter level 1 with the use of the 3 to 1 Method. Tell yourself mentally that you are going to count from 1 to 3, and at the count of 3 you will open your eyes and read the lesson. Mention the lesson title and subject.

Add: "Noises will not distract me, but will help me to concentrate. I will have superior concentration and understanding."

Count from 1 to 3, open your eyes, and read the lesson.

When you have read the lesson, once again enter level 1 with the 3 to 1 Method. Tell yourself mentally, "I will recall the lesson I have just read (mention title and subject) anytime in the future with the use of the Three Fingers Technique."

To hear a lecture, enter level 1 with the 3 to 1 Method, and tell yourself mentally that you are going to hear a lecture and mention the title, subject, and lecturer's name.

Tell yourself that you are going to use the Three Fingers Technique. Keep your eyes open during the lecture.

Tell yourself that noises will not distract you, but will help you to concentrate; that you will have superior concentration and understanding; and that you will recall the lecture (mention title, subject, and lecturer's name) anytime in the future with the use of the Three Fingers Technique.

For test taking with the Three Fingers Technique, follow the Three Cycle Method.

First: Read your test questions the way you always do, but do not stay too long on any of them. If you have a ready answer, put it down; if not, skip that question, and move to the next one.

Second: Use the Three Fingers Technique and do as in the first cycle, but stay a little longer on the unanswered question.

When an answer comes, put it down; if not, skip that question, and move to the next one.

Third: Use the Three Fingers Technique, read the unanswered question, and if still no answer comes, close your eyes, turn them slightly upward, visualize or imagine your professor on your Mental Screen, and ask for the answer. Then clear your mind, and start thinking again to figure out the answer. The answer that comes is your professor's. Write it down. Do not turn in a blank paper.

Mirror of the Mind

We will now impress information for your benefit, programming the Mirror of the Mind, a formula-type technique you can use for problem solving.

Create and project on your Mental Screen a full-length mirror. This mirror will be known as the Mirror of the Mind.

This Mirror of the Mind can be mentally increased in size to encompass within its frame, a thing or things, a person or persons, a small scene or a large scene.

The color of the frame of the Mirror of the Mind can be mentally changed from blue to white. The blue frame will denote the problem, or the existing situation, which can be converted into a project; the white frame will denote the solution, or goal.

To solve a problem or to reach a goal with the Mirror of the Mind, enter level 1 with the 3 to 1 Method, then project the image of the Mirror of the Mind with blue frame on your Mental Screen.

Create an image of the problem, thing, person, or scene, and project it on your blue-framed Mirror of the Mind, in order to make a good study of the problem.

After making a good study of the problem, erase the problem image, move the mirror to your left, change the mirror's frame to white, and create and project a solution image onto the white-framed mirror.

From then on, any time you happen to think of the project, visualize the solution image you have created, framed in white. And this is so.

I will now allow time for you to work one problem case. Begin by applying your learned techniques. When you hear my voice again, you will relax even more. (pause)

Mental Rehearsal

We will now impress information for your benefit, programming the Mental Rehearsal Technique, a formula-type technique that you can use to help you improve your physical performance.

When you have an activity to perform and you desire to rehearse it mentally ahead of time, enter level 1 with the 3 to 1 Method, and then project yourself mentally to the location where you will perform the activity.

Once you have projected yourself mentally to the place where you will perform the activity, imagine yourself performing the way you desire. Imagine yourself improving, and accomplishing your task successfully.

Notice how you feel as you are performing the task. Imagine how you feel as you begin the activity the way that you desire. Imagine how you feel as you progress in the activity. Imagine feeling successful, and imagine a sense of accomplishment as you succeed at your assigned task.

I will now allow you time to practice your learned techniques. When you hear my voice again, you will relax even more. (Pause)

Weight and Habit Control

We will now impress and program Habit Control, formula-type techniques you can use to control the eating and smoking habits.

Formula-type technique for Habit Control, Weight: When you desire to reduce weight, enter level 1 by the use of the 3 to 1 Method, and analyze your weight problem. At level 1, mentally mark a big red NO over every item of food considered to be causing the problem.

Program yourself that hunger between meals will vanish by eating a piece of carrot, celery, or apple, or some such helpful foods, or by taking three deep breaths.

Program yourself to leave something on your plate, realizing that you do not need all the food you have taken. Program yourself not to eat dessert.

Visualize yourself in the blue-framed Mirror of the Mind the way you are now. Then, in the white-framed mirror, stamp what you want to weigh on one corner and the size of suit or dress you want to wear on the other corner, and imagine yourself at your ideal weight and size.

Thereafter, when you think of your weight, always visualize the image you have created of yourself the way you want to be in the white-framed Mirror of the Mind.

Whenever you are eating, visualize the image you have created of yourself the way you want to look in the white-framed Mirror of the Mind, and visualize your desired weight stamped on one corner and your desired size of clothing stamped on the other corner.

If you desire to gain weight, eat those foods that you sense at level 1 will help you gain; eat slowly, savoring every bite. Learn to improve your taste and smell by concentrating on your food as you eat.

Use the Mirror of the Mind and visualize yourself the way you want to be; do this every time you think of your weight.

Formula-type techniques for Habit Control, Smoking. Whenever you wish to reduce or discontinue cigarette smoking, enter level 1 by the 3 to 1 Method, and at level 1 analyze the problem.

Determine when you smoke the first cigarette of the day, then program yourself at level 1 to smoke it one hour later. When that becomes effective, program yourself to smoke the first cigarette still one hour later, and continue to make these changes by programming at level 1 until you smoke only a few cigarettes a day; it will then be a simple matter to stop smoking altogether.

You can also program yourself to smoke only one cigarette per hour on the hour; when this has become effective, then program yourself to smoke only on the even hours. After this has taken effect, it will be a simple matter to stop smoking completely.

You can also program yourself at level 1 to stop smoking altogether thirty days from the date of your initial programming.

You can mark a date on a calendar thirty days from the present, and tell yourself mentally that on this date you will stop smoking and never smoke again in your life. Reinforce this programming for this purpose at level 1 daily, and this will be so.

Tips that help in your programming at level 1 to stop smoking:
- Change brands frequently.
- Do not inhale the cigarette smoke.

- Program that three deep breaths will stop the immediate desire to smoke.
- Stop smoking for the sake of your loved ones.

Mental Mentor

We will now impress information for your benefit, programming the Mental Mentor technique.

At this time, think of a person that you admire, someone who has helped you and taught you and guided you in your life or your career. (pause) You can use your memory of this person as a Mental Mentor.

Now create and project onto your Mental Screen a mental picture of this person who has helped you, this person who is one of your favorite teachers. (pause) Recall what this person looks like: their height and weight (pause), their facial features (pause), the color and length of their hair. (pause) Recall how this person moves, their gestures; (pause) recall how this person talks. (pause)

Now imagine your Mental Mentor moving away from the Mental Screen and becoming dynamic and fully alive. (pause)

It is now an accomplished fact that you have created a spiritual duplicate of your favorite teacher. This spiritual duplicate that you have created will be known as your Mental Mentor.

You can imagine talking with your Mental Mentor at any time and imagine how your Mentor would guide you and support you and serve as an example for you. Your Mental Mentor can encourage you when you are performing tasks. Simply recall your Mental Mentor, and imagine what he or she would say to you, and use this to help you achieve greater results.

Reader: When you have finished reading the formula-type technique/s you want to impress, then continue with the next section (below).

Post Effects, Preview of Next Session

You have practiced entering deep, healthy levels of mind. In your next session you will again enter level 1, and you will enter a deeper, healthier level of mind faster and easier than this time.

When you take the next step, and continue with the Silva ESP training, you will begin to establish subjective points of reference with the use of mental projection at the PSI "EXTRA SENSE" levels, the Effective Sensory Projection levels for your success.

Post Effects, Standard

Every time you function at these levels of the mind, you will receive beneficial effects physically and mentally.

You may use these levels of the mind to help yourself physically and mentally.

You may use these levels of the mind to help your loved ones physically and mentally.

You may use these levels of the mind to help any human being who needs help physically and mentally.

You will never use these levels of the mind to harm any human being; if this be your intention, you will not be able to function within these levels of the mind.

You will always use these levels of the mind in a constructive, creative manner for all that is good, honest, pure, clean, and positive. And this is so.

You will continue to strive to take part in constructive and creative activities to make this a better world to live in, so that when we move on, we shall have left behind a better world for those who follow. You will consider the whole of humanity, depending on their ages, as fathers or mothers, brothers or sisters, sons or daughters. You are a superior human being; you have greater understanding, compassion, and patience with others.

Bring Out

In a moment, I am going to count from 1 to 5. At that moment, you will open your eyes, be wide awake, feeling fine and in perfect health, feeling better than before. You will have no ill effects whatsoever in your head, no headache; no ill effects whatsoever in your hearing, no buzzing in your ears; no ill effects whatsoever in your vision and eyesight; vision, eyesight, and hearing improve every time you function at these levels of mind.

1–2, coming out slowly now.

3, at the count of 5, you will open your eyes, be wide awake, feeling fine and in perfect health, feeling better than before, feeling the way you feel when you have slept the right amount of revitalizing, refreshing, relaxing, healthy sleep.

4–5. Eyes open, wide awake, feeling fine and in perfect health, feeling better than before.

Appendix D

Hand Levitation and Glove Anesthesia Conditioning Cycle

(Reader: Do not read the headings out loud.)

Deepening

I will now review briefly how to enter level 1 with the Hand Levitation method.

When we begin, you will assume an erect sitting position, allowing yourself enough room to raise your arm comfortably. Then you will look at and concentrate on your stronger hand while both hands rest on your lap, palms down. While I count slowly from 10 to 1, you will go through a complete cycle of hand levitation. When I reach the count of 1, the back of your hand will contact your face, and you will enter a deeper, healthier level of mind. I will be giving you directions on each descending number when we begin the count.

Now assume a comfortable, erect sitting position; place your hands on your lap, palms down. Keep your eyes open, and do not close them until the back of your hand touches your face. I will give you directions on each number.

10—Look at your stronger hand. Keep your eyes focused on your hand. (pause)

9—Cause your hand to feel sensitive, very sensitive. Slowly cause one finger to move, then cause your fingers to separate from one another, and at the same time cause your hand to rise from your lap. (pause)

8—Continue to allow your hand to rise in the direction of your face. (pause)

7—Higher and higher. Feel your arm becoming lighter and lighter as the back of your hand draws closer and closer to your face. Your hand may feel as though a balloon is lifting it. (pause)

6—Allow your hand and arm to become still lighter and lighter as you continue to help them rise higher and higher. (pause)

5—They become lighter and lighter as you allow your hand and arm to rise higher and higher, now beyond the midpoint between your face and your lap. (pause)

4—Raise them higher and higher. When I reach the count of 1, you will have entered level 1, the basic plane level. (pause)

3—Your hand and arm rise higher and higher and become lighter and lighter, now drawing very near your face. (pause)

2—You are now beginning to enter the basic plane level. (pause)

1—The back of your hand now touches your face. Close your eyes, take a deep breath, and while exhaling, return your hand to its resting position on your lap. (pause)

You are now at a deeper, healthier level of mind, deeper than before.

Deepening (Routine Cycle)

To help you enter a deeper, healthier level of mind, I am going to count from 10 to 1. On each descending number, you will feel yourself going deeper, and you will enter a deeper, healthier level of mind.

10—9, feel going deeper,

8—7—6, deeper and deeper,

5—4—3, deeper and deeper,

2—1

You are now at a deeper, healthier level of mind, deeper than before.

You may enter a deeper, healthier level of mind by simply relaxing your eyelids. Relax your eyelids. (pause) Feel how relaxed they are. (pause) Allow this feeling of relaxation to flow slowly downward throughout your body, all the way down to your toes. (pause)

It is a wonderful feeling to be deeply relaxed, a very healthy state of being.

To help you enter a deeper, healthier level of mind, I am going to count from 1 to 3. At that moment, you will project yourself mentally to your ideal place of relaxation. I will then stop talking to you, and when you next hear my voice, one hour of time will have elapsed at this level of mind. My voice will not startle you; you will take a deep breath, relax, and go deeper.

1—(pause)—2—(pause)—3. Project yourself mentally to your ideal place of relaxation until you hear my voice again. Relax. (Reader: Remain silent for about thirty seconds.)

Relax. (pause) Take a deep breath, and as you exhale, relax and go deeper. (pause)

Rapport

You will continue to listen to my voice; you will continue to follow the instructions at this level of the mind and any other level, including the outer conscious level. This is for your benefit; you desire it, and it is so.

Whenever you mentally or verbally mention the word "Relax," all unnecessary movements and activities of your body, brain, and mind will cease immediately, and you will become completely passive and relaxed physically and mentally.

I may bring you out of this level or a deeper level than this by counting to you from 1 to 5. At the count of 5, your eyes will open; you will be wide awake, feeling fine and in perfect health.

Genius Statements

The difference between genius mentality and lay mentality is that geniuses use more of their minds and use them in a special manner.

You are now learning to use more of your mind and to use it in a special manner.

Beneficial Statements

The following are beneficial statements that you may occasionally repeat while at these levels of the mind. Repeat mentally after me. (Reader: Read slowly.)

My increasing mental faculties are for serving humanity better.

Every day, in every way, I am getting better, better, and better.

Positive thoughts bring me benefits and advantages I desire.

I have full control and complete dominion over my sensing faculties at this level of the mind and any other level, including the outer conscious level. And this is so.

Preventive Statements

The following preventive statements are for your better health. Keep in mind that from now on, I will occasionally be speaking in your place. (Read slowly.)

I will never learn to develop, physically or mentally, mental disorders nor psychosomatic or functional ailments or diseases.

I will never learn to develop, physically or mentally, a dependence on drugs or alcohol.

Negative thoughts and negative suggestions have no influence over me at any level of the mind.

I will always maintain a perfectly healthy body and mind.

Mental Projection Statements for Success

I am now learning to attune my intelligence by developing my sensing faculties, and to project them to any problem area, so as to become aware of any abnormalities, if this is necessary and beneficial for humanity.

I am now learning to apply corrective measures and to correct any abnormality I detect.

Negative thoughts and negative suggestions have no influence over me at any level of the mind.

Impression of New Material, Programming

Impression of information for your benefit, programming: We have impressed and programmed how to enter level 1 with the Hand Levitation method. You may use Hand Levitation to enter deeper, healthier programming levels. Remember: Every time you practice Hand Levitation, you will enter deeper levels of mind.

Glove Anesthesia

Glove Anesthesia, a formula-type technique that you can practice to develop control of physiological pain and in many cases control of bleeding and hemorrhaging.

Glove Anesthesia is the development of a feeling that is different from the normal and usually developed on the less strong of the two hands.

It could be a cool or cold feeling, or a feeling such as a tingling sensation, a vibration, as though your hand is asleep, as though you have a leather glove on your hand, as though your hand is made of wood, as though you have no hand; any feeling other than the normal will be considered to be Glove Anesthesia.

In a moment I am going to count from 1 to 3; at that moment you will place your stronger hand into an imaginary container of hot water standing by your side; the water is hot and you can stand the temperature. 1-2-3. Now place your hand into the imaginary container of hot water by your side. (pause) Bring back a memory when you had your hand in hot water before, any time you can recall vividly. (pause) Now lift your hand out of the hot water and let it rest on your lap. (pause)

I will now count from 1 to 3; at that moment you will place your other hand into a container of ice water with cracked ice, standing by your side. 1-2-3. Now place your hand into the imaginary container of ice water with cracked ice standing by your side. (pause) Recall a time when you had your hand in ice water. (pause) Feel the ice water and cracked ice between your fingers. (pause) Feel your hand icy cold. (pause)

While your hand is getting colder and colder every second, let us review the first ten memory pegs to improve visualization by using the Mental Screen. Number 1, the letter T, the word "Tea." Project it on your Mental Screen, a picture of a glass of tea. (pause) Number 2, the letter N, the word "Noah." Project on your Mental Screen a picture of a man with a long white beard. (pause) Number 3, the letter M, the word "May." Project a mental picture of a calendar on your screen. (pause) Number 4, the letter R, the word "Ray," mental picture: sun rays. (pause) Number 5, the letter L, the word "Law," mental picture: a policeman. (pause) Number 6, the letter J, the word "Jaw," mental picture: a man with a large jaw. (pause) Number 7, the letter K, the word "Key," mental picture: a large gold key. (pause) Number 8, the letter F, the word "Fee," mental picture: a price tag of 8 million dollars. (pause) Number 9, the letter B, the word "Bay," mental picture: land and water. (pause) Number 10, the letters T and S, the word "Toes," mental picture: ten toes. (pause)

Now, keeping your eyes closed, lift your hand out of the ice water, and place it over and behind your head, keeping your hand from touching your head. (pause) Let your hand dry and get colder in this position. I will tell you when to bring it down. Continue to keep your eyes closed.

As soon as you learn to develop Glove Anesthesia, and after testing it and becoming satisfied with the results, start practicing the transferring of this anesthesia to other parts of the body. First practice transferring this anesthesia from one hand to the other by placing the anesthetized hand over the other hand for a few seconds; then test the other hand for anesthesia.

When this has become effective, practice transferring the anesthesia from either hand to any other part of the body. This is done by placing either hand over that part of the body and holding it in that position for a few seconds. Finally you can learn, by practicing, to program yourself so that by concentrating on any discomfort and mentally saying the word "Gone," the discomfort will be gone.

Now bring your hand down, place it on your lap, and test it for coldness and insensibility with your other hand. (pause) Now remove all abnormal feeling from your hand by rubbing it three times with your other hand, from the wrist toward the fingers, bringing all feeling back to normal. (pause) Your hand now feels as it did before the exercise.

You may reinforce the effects of this formula by practice.

To correct health problems, controls are applied under a doctor's supervision.

Post Effects; Preview of Next Session

You have practiced entering deep, healthy levels of mind. In your next session, you will again enter level 1, and you will enter a deeper, healthier level of mind faster and easier than this time.

Post Effects: Standard

Every time you function at these levels of the mind, you will receive beneficial effects physically and mentally.

You may use these levels of the mind to help yourself, physically and mentally.

You may use these levels of the mind to help your loved ones, physically and mentally.

You may use these levels of the mind to help any human being who needs help, physically and mentally.

You will never use these levels of the mind to harm any human being; if this be your intention, you will not be able to function within these levels of the mind.

You will always use these levels of the mind in a constructive, creative manner for all that is good, honest, pure, clean, and positive. And this is so.

You will continue to strive to take part in constructive and creative activities to make this a better world to live in, so that when we move on, we shall have left behind a better world for those who follow. You will consider the whole of humanity, depending on their ages, as fathers or mothers, brothers or sisters, sons or daughters. You are a superior human being; you have greater understanding, compassion, and patience with others.

Bring Out

In a moment, I am going to count from 1 to 5. At that moment, you will open your eyes, be wide awake, feeling fine and in perfect health, feeling better than before. You will have no ill effects whatsoever in your head, no headache; no ill effects whatsoever in your hearing, no buzzing in your ears; no ill effects whatsoever in your vision and eyesight; vision, eyesight, and hearing improve every time you function at these levels of mind.

1-2, coming out slowly now.

3, at the count of 5, you will open your eyes, be wide awake, feeling fine and in perfect health, feeling better than before, feeling the way you feel when you have slept the right amount of revitalizing, refreshing, relaxing, healthy sleep.

4-5. Eyes open, wide awake, feeling fine and in perfect health, feeling better than before.

Appendix E

Resources and Contact Information

FREE INTRODUCTORY LESSONS AND VIDEOS
SilvaESP.com/csv/

SPECIAL OFFER
As an owner of this book, you can get the audio version of this course and our other home study courses at a discount. Visit SilvaESP.com and submit the coupon code SuccessBook when you check out.

INFORMATION ABOUT SILVA COURSES AND PRODUCTS
SilvaESP.com.

ECUMENICAL SOCIETY HOLISTIC FAITH HEALING WEBSITE
ESPsy.org

HELP FOR HEALTH PROBLEMS
If you have a health problem and want Silva ESP graduates to program for you, or if you are a Silva ESP graduate and want health cases to work, please visit this website: SilvaHealthCases.com

CPSIA information can be obtained
at www.ICGtesting.com
Printed in the USA
JSHW060800160922
30538JS00003B/7